Do the RIGHT THING

Jane Goldman is the author of nine books, including four for young adults and two number one best-sellers. She also works as a screenwriter and producer. She lives in London with her husband, three children, four dogs, three cats, several ferrets, a snake called Ken and an iguana called Dave.

Jane Goldman

Do the RIGHT THING

A Teenager's Guide To Surviving Any Social Situation

PICCADILLY PRESS • LONDON

For Betty, Harvey and Honey

This edition revised and updated 2007

First published in Great Britain in 1995 under the title
For Weddings, A Funeral and When You Can't Flush the Loo
by Piccadilly Press, 5 Castle Road, London NW1 8PR

A catalogue record for this book is available
from the British Library

ISBN: 978 1 85340 894 6 (trade paperback)

1 3 5 7 9 10 8 6 4 2

Printed and bound by Bookmarque Ltd
Designed and typeset by M Rules, London
Cover design by Simon Davis

Contents

Home and Away

Socialising

Eating

Parties

Special Occasions

Out and About

Work and Interviews

Introduction

Over the twelve years since this book was first published, I've received so many lovely letters from readers who have found it useful. But it was only when, while working on a movie last summer, one of my colleagues brought in his well-thumbed original copy and very kindly told me that it had been his bible all through his teenage years, that I realised that the first wave of readers had, in fact, grown up. I'm not sure why this hadn't occurred to me before - after all, when I wrote it I was a young mum, frantically scribbling away during my two children's nap-times, and now I have two teenagers and a ten-year-old and seem to have started needing an afternoon nap myself, so you'd think I might have noticed the passage of time!

Anyway, by a huge coincidence, it was just a couple of days later that I got an email suggesting a revised and updated edition, which – as you'll have guessed, given that you're holding a copy in your hands right now - I thought was a great idea.

I hope you find it entertaining and interesting and, most importantly, useful.

Jane Goldman
2007

Dating

Asking for a Date

It wasn't so very long ago that it was completely unheard of for a girl to ask a boy for a date. It was an unfair, frustrating situation for everyone – for the boys, who had to do all the running around and risk rejection, and for the girls who had to sit around like lemons, waiting and hoping for guys they fancied to ask them out. Girls are now getting a taste of the asking-for-a-date jitters that boys have known about all along. Let's face it: asking for a date is scary. Everyone feels shy. Everyone is frightened of getting turned down. And everyone wants to hear the girl or guy of their dreams saying yes. You're more likely to get the result you want – or at least to come out of the whole experience happy, unconfused and with your pride intact – if you remember these important guidelines:

Ask in person

It can be tempting to persuade a mate to set you up with someone, especially if you're super-shy, or can't bear the thought of getting turned down to your face. This can work out fine if your would-be date knows all about you and is very keen to go out with you. But if they're not one hundred per cent sure, they're more likely to say no than they would be if you asked them out yourself. They may wonder why you didn't ask yourself. Couldn't you be bothered? Were you embarrassed to be seen talking to them? Or maybe they'll think it's all a big joke your mates are playing on you and you don't know anything about it . . . If your would-be date hardly knows you, it's even worse: they don't know what you're like, and might assume that you're aloof or snotty or a complete and utter scaredy-cat. Or you might be lazy, into bossing your friends around or perhaps have an astonishingly silly voice that you're embarrassed to let anyone hear.

Bottom line: you'll make a better impression, and have a better chance of getting a yes if you ask in person.

If you're really too shy to ask for a date face to face, or you just can't get a good opportunity to do it, a phonecall is fine. A text or email is OK too, but do bear in mind that the advantage of asking in person or by phone is that you'll always get an answer one way or another, whereas sending a text or mail will leave you nervously waiting for a reply! And if you do decide to phone, remember that the same goes for voicemail – better to just leave a message saying you've called, and leave the actual asking out until you speak in person.

Have good timing

The better your timing, the better your chances. For the best results, don't ask someone for a date when they're surrounded by their friends (they might be embarrassed, or act tough and dismissive just to impress their mates), or when you're surrounded by yours (they might think it's a joke, that you're showing off, or that you're a gutless sap to need all that moral support). Don't ask when someone seems moody or distracted (they might have a crisis on and not want to even think about dates) or immediately after they've had some great triumph (they might think you're an easily-impressed idiot who wasn't interested before, but has suddenly perked up at the slightest hint of glory). Don't ask immediately after being turned down by someone else (no one likes to think they're someone's second choice).

Be direct and to the point

The best way to ask for a date is to be really specific, e.g. 'Do you fancy going to the cinema with me this Friday?' If you mess about, asking vague things like, 'Do you like films?', you're just dragging out the conversation and putting off the big moment when you actually have to get to the point. After all, perhaps the object of your affections loves movies, but wouldn't want to go on a date with you, or would love to go out with you, but doesn't like movies. Saying: 'Would you like to go out with me sometime?' isn't much better, because it puts your would-be date on the spot, and sets you up for a horribly big put-down. I mean, do you really want to be told, no? Inviting someone on a specific date is by far your best option. If they want to go out with you, they'll say yes. If they want to but can't make that date, they'll tell you. And if they don't want to go out with you at all, they'll be able to let you down in a much gentler way which will be easier for both of you.

Give plenty of notice . . .

Don't expect a yes if you ask someone for a date tonight or tomorrow – they've probably got plans. Ask at least two days in advance.

. . . but not too much

Don't be tempted, however, to ask someone for a first date way in advance (i.e. ten days, two weeks). Sure, they're probably free, but if they do want to go out with you, they'll wonder why on earth you don't want to go out sooner, and if they don't they're in a terrible spot and will be left with no choice but to give you a straightforward brush-off, which will be horrible for both of you.

Be casual . . .

The more laid-back you are, the less embarrassing the whole experience will be for you and your would-be date. For instance, it would be a bad idea to say, 'I'm deeply, desperately in love with you and I want to go on a date with you', or confess to having watched or followed someone for any length of time. You will seem scary and mad and your chosen one will not especially want to go anywhere with you, except perhaps to a nice, secure unit where some friendly men in white coats will help you into a straitjacket. Being eager is cute and flattering, as long as you keep it to a reasonable level. The mere fact that you're asking for a date clearly says I like you – there's no need to go overboard.

. . . but not too casual

Some people make the mistake of being ridiculously dismissive or even a bit mean, to cover themselves in case they get turned down. This is rude, confusing and pointless, and you'll be more likely to get turned down if you do it.

Be confident

Being shy is fine – everybody is shy to different degrees, and nobody is going to be put off by a little shyness. However, people do get put off by doormat behaviour, and if you put yourself down, people tend to agree with you. In other words, if you say, 'I don't suppose a wonderful, popular, good-looking type like you would ever want to go out with someone as geeky as me, but . . .' your would-be date is unlikely to leap at the chance to date you.

Are there any special pointers for asking people out by phone?

The basic rules are the same, but it's also worth remembering to:

- **Call at a time that's hopefully good for your would-be date**
  Avoid calling early in the morning (when everyone is rushing to get ready for the day), late at night (you don't want to wake anyone up), during usual mealtimes and at times when there's something extremely exciting or important on telly.

- **Call at a time that's good for you**
  If you call when you're late for something, have a dodgy mobile phone signal, have other stuff on your mind or are likely to be disturbed, you'll be fidgety and distracted. You should also be alone when you call. Don't let your mates persuade you to call and ask someone out while they're there, even if they promise to keep quiet. They probably won't manage it, and your would-be date is unlikely to be impressed by raucous, matey giggling in the background. Worse still, they might assume that you're only calling for a bet or a joke or to show off.

- **If you're calling a landline, be very polite to whoever answers**
  If your date's parents or siblings think you sound nice, it can be a big bonus.

- **Ask right away if you've called at an OK time**
  If your would-be date is up to their ears in homework or watching their favourite show on TV, they might not be as receptive to your invitation as they could be.

- **Avoid long, painful silences**
  Some people find that it helps to scribble themselves a few
  notes outlining what they want to say. A word of warning,
  though: only use your notes as a prompt; if you read them
  out word for word, like a script, you'll sound strange.

If you're asking someone out at the last minute
because someone else has let you down, should
you explain the situation to them?

Hmmm, tricky. No one wants to be told that they're a last
resort, but it's better to be honest than to lie and be caught
out. And you could well be caught out – anyone with half a
brain would be suspicious of a last-minute invitation anyway,
and then there's always the chance that some tactless loser will
come up to you when you're out and say something stupid,
like, 'Hey – I thought you were supposed to be meeting so-
and-so!'. Either way, then, asking someone out as a
last-minute substitute could mean blowing your chances with
them for good. If you don't care, then go ahead. But if you
really like them, it would be wiser to go dateless for an
evening and ask them out another time, when they're your
first choice.

Getting Asked Out

Getting asked out is obviously nowhere near as scary as doing
the asking yourself, but make no mistake: the way you handle
it matters, a lot. Whether you're accepting an invitation or turning it down, doing it right counts. Botch the job, and people
can get confused, put-off or offended; then they can scamper
off and say things which could put other people off asking you
out. Do it right, and everyone is happy. Here's how:

Be clear

If you're thrilled to be asked out, show it. Smile. Say thanks. Say you'd love to go. If you can't go, say why not, and suggest a day when you are free. That way your would-be date knows you're genuinely unable to go and not just giving them the brush-off.

Be helpful and encouraging

If someone asks you whether you'd fancy a date sometime, they're probably pretty unsure of themselves, so it's nice to help them out. If you like the idea, ask when they're free, suggest a date yourself, or just offer to swap phone numbers – anything to get the ball rolling. If you don't like the idea, let them down gently (see below).

Don't keep people hanging on, if you can help it

There might be times when you're not one hundred per cent sure whether you want to go on a date or not. However, it's pretty mean to keep someone dangling, waiting for your answer. You should really say yes or no to a date as soon as you're asked, but if you're desperate to buy some time to think it over, you can ask for someone's number and promise to call and let them know. But you've got to call within a couple of days, max.

Be kind

If you don't want to go out – not this week, not ever – you've got to be blunt, but kind at the same time. Saying, 'It's so nice of you to ask, but no thanks . . .' is blunt but friendly. Saying, 'What? Me and you? You're kidding!? Hahahahaha! Never!' is also blunt, but will make you seem like a horrible person – which you're not, are you? You don't need to explain why you don't want to date someone, but if you feel you want to, stick to straightforward excuses, such as, 'I'm afraid I'm already seeing someone and I don't think they'd be very pleased if I went on a date with someone else!'. 'I like you as a friend, but . . .' is also OK, as long as you really do like them as a friend – it would be mean to say this to someone you didn't actually want to see at all. Avoid excuses like, 'I don't think it would work out' (the person asking you out obviously won't agree) or 'I don't really want to date anyone at the moment' (if you do go out with someone else in the near future, you'll look like a horrible fibber).

Be discreet

If you want to be popular, likeable and well-thought-of, don't be a blabbermouth. Of course, it's fine to tell your friends that you're off on a date. But if you sound off to everyone who'll listen and basically do everything to make news of your impending date as widespread as possible, short of taking out a full-page ad in the local paper, you could end up embarrassing your date and putting them off you before you've even been out.

The no-blabbing rule counts double if you've turned down a date. The person who asked you out may have been a disgusting gimboid, but no one deserves to have their failures broadcast to the world at large. Would you like everyone to know if you'd been turned down? Not a lot. Even if you couldn't care less about other people's feelings, you should consider your own image. If you make the brush-off public knowledge, you'll seem hard-nosed and thoughtless, and prospective dates will be far less likely to take a chance on asking you out in the future, in case you give them the same knock-back-followed-by-public-announcement treatment.

How can you politely get rid of someone who keeps asking you out, even after you've turned them down?

If you're not clear when you turn someone down, you can't blame them for persisting. Saying, 'I'm sorry, but I'm busy all week,' may seem like a big brush-off to you, but to someone who is crazy about you, it just means that you're not free until next week. Most people will get the right message if you say thanks-but-no-thanks, and don't give any excuse about why you can't go. It's polite, it's friendly and it usually works.

If you've been clear all along, and are still getting bugged, it's not out of order to be a little firmer. It's quite OK to say, 'Look, it's very nice of you to keep asking me out, but I'm afraid I'm going to say no again'. If you look serious while you say it, there should be no doubt about what you mean.

The Dating Game

Every game has its rules, and it's always worth knowing them before you wade in and start playing – especially if you want to be a winner, and get asked to play again . . .

How much notice should you give if you have to cancel a date?

As much as you possibly can – in other words, the minute you know you won't be able to make it. Remember that it's rude to cancel a date. You should only do it if it's completely unavoidable. Cancelling on the day of the date is a bit mean, because it leaves your date no time to make alternative plans, so he or she might well be stuck in alone with nothing to do. If you have to (e.g. you're ill or your parents are making you stay in), get in touch as early in the day as possible.

When you cancel a date, you should always apologise like mad, give a very clear explanation and arrange a new date.

Is it ever OK to stand someone up?

Never, ever, ever! The only passable excuse is if you have a huge personal tragedy. Otherwise, if you can't make a date for any reason, you have got to get in touch with your date and cancel. If you can't get hold of them in person, and you're in any doubt about whether they'll get a chance to pick up a voicemail or text, you should really go. If you simply can't go, you should send someone in your place to tell your date that you won't be coming along.

What should you do if someone stands you up?

Get hold of them and give them a serious mouthful! If they invite you on another date, think carefully before accepting. Being stood up is insulting and humiliating, and you deserve better.

What should you do if you or your date are late?

Check out the *Out and About* section on p.164 for the low-down on lateness.

Who should pay for a date?

In the past, the theory was always that the person who did the asking – male or female – should expect to pay. This was fine for adults on a weekly wage, but quite a strain on hard-up teenagers! These days, most people expect to go dutch (pay half each) for a coffee, a meal, a trip to the cinema or whatever. So if you've been asked out, you should always offer to pay half, and not assume that the person who asked you is going to foot the bill. If you've done the asking, and can afford to offer to pay for your date too, then it's certainly a nice gesture and sure to be appreciated, but if you can't, it shouldn't be a problem. However, if you're inviting someone to a gig, comedy show or some other expensive event, you should always make it clear when you're asking for the date whether or not you expect to go halves. Asking someone if they fancy going to see a particular show with you suggests that you already have two tickets, and while it's normal to split a bill during a date, it's a bit dodgy to ask your date to hand you money for something you've already paid for, and it could be much more than they can afford! If you can't stretch to buying a second ticket to an event, always make it crystal clear when you're inviting someone out that you're expecting them to pay – you should say how much the tickets are, check if that's OK, and tell your date that you'll buy the tickets and they can pay you back on the night.

What happens if you've got no money at all?

It shouldn't be a hassle as long as you explain your situation right away. If someone asks you out, there's nothing wrong with saying, 'I'd love to come, but I'm afraid I'm broke right now . . . ' Hopefully your date will offer to pay. If they can't afford it, at least they've been warned, and can plan a cheap or cost-free date.

Obviously it's a bit trickier if you're broke and you want to do the asking – you can't ask someone to take you out and pay for you. You can still ask them as long as you come clean right away and invite them on a date where you won't need cash. How about going for a walk or a bike ride, or spending an evening in watching a DVD at your place?

Are all the old-fashioned dating rules out the window? Or are boys still meant to open doors for their date, pull chairs out for them to sit on, help them take their coat or jacket off, etc?

Any rules which are specifically for boys are probably well past their sell-by date. There's no good reason why boys should behave like glorified servants while girls have to stand around acting like vegetables. In reality, both boys and girls should make every effort to treat their date nicely, and both have every right to expect the same treatment back. Here are some good, common-sense dating rules for everybody:

- Whoever is nearest to a door should open it and hold it open.
- If your date is struggling with their jacket, help them to put it on or take it off (ideally whichever action they were trying to perform – or else it could be annoying!).
- If you run into people you know while you're out, always introduce them to your date.
- If you're out in a group, never ignore your date, boss them around or get them to do things for you just to impress your friends.
- Holding hands or linking arms is lovely, but be sensible about it – don't desperately cling on to your date the whole time.
- If your date does something courteous for you, don't take the mick or say you can do it yourself – it's unfair to embarrass someone who is trying to be nice.
- Don't do anything else that might make your date feel

stupid or embarrassed. If they say something dumb, ignore it. If they do something dumb – like walk into a lamp-post or spill food down themselves – hold back the giggles, shrug and say something reassuring, like, 'Y'know, that happens to me all the time!'.

What should I do if I do something stupid?

Ideally, you should just make a little joke, then try to forget it. If you go on and on about it, your date could start to feel horribly embarrassed for you, you'll both feel uncomfortable, and the whole mood will be ruined.

What if they want to go on another date and you don't?

If your date likes you, but you don't like them, it's tricky when they ask you for another date. As with any brush-off, be kind and gentle but crystal clear. 'I've really had fun, and it was very nice to meet you, but no thank you . . .' is fine.

Group Dating

The most important rule for successful group dating is to think about everyone on the date – not just yourself and your partner – and make sure that everyone has a good time.

Is it OK to have a private chat with your date?

Yes, as long as it's quick and doesn't make the rest of the group feel left out. Whispering is a no-no, and so are long, deep, intense conversations. Basically, you shouldn't ignore everyone else for any length of time, unless they seem to want to chat in pairs too.

Is it OK to snog on a group date?

It can be, but you should be super-cautious and thoughtful. If your date seems uncomfortable, then obviously you should give it a miss. Also bear in mind that even if both of you are in the mood to get smoochy your companions might not be and will find it embarrassing. Worse still, if one half of another couple is keen to get intimate and the other half isn't, the keen one could use your snogging as a tool for pressuring their partner, saying, 'Well look, they're doing it, so . . .'.

Is it rude to break away from a group date if you want to be alone with your date?

To be honest, it would make more sense to go out alone together in the first place. But if the others in the group are in a different mood from you and your date – i.e. you're getting smoochy when they just want to have fun, or vice versa – it makes more sense to break away than to stick around and do your own thing regardless.

Blind Dates

A blind date – where two people who have never met before are set up – can be a wonderful experience or a horrible one. These days, many people also find themselves invited on semi-blind dates, where you may have met a friend-of-a-friend online – perhaps on MSN or a social networking site like Myspace or Bebo – and been asked out by them, but not yet met them in person. Here are some tips:

- Obviously, safety should be your first concern. You should never consider meeting up with someone unless a friend or relative of yours knows them very, very well. Even then, you should never meet up with them alone.

- The most painless blind dates are the kind where a boy and a girl who are a couple go on a date and each bring a single friend along to introduce to each other. The more people there are on the date, the easier it is for the blind-daters – at least if they discover that they find each other difficult to talk to, they can talk to someone else.

- Better still is to organise an opportunity for the two people being set up to meet each other in a relaxed, friendly group situation – that way they get a chance to decide whether they like each other enough to want to go on a date some other time!

- Even if you're certain there are no safety issues, blind dates where the daters meet up and go out alone are best avoided. You don't want to get stuck in an awkward situation where you discover that you've got absolutely nothing in common apart from the fact that you both wish you weren't there!

- The above warning still counts even if you've chatted to your prospective date online or on the phone and got along well. Chatting anonymously is a lot easier than chatting in person, and it's amazing how weird it can be to find yourself face-to-face with someone you barely know. But if you're utterly determined to do a just-the-two-of-you blind date, it's a good idea to plan a very short one – just a coffee in a café, say, instead of a whole evening or day out. That way you can suggest going on somewhere else if you're having a good time, or politely escape if it's a nightmare. (This is also a good tip for any first date, if you don't know your date very well.)

- If you're disappointed by your blind date's appearance

when they show up, try to hide it. It's rude and mean to say things like, 'I was expecting you to be taller' or 'Wow, you really look different to your Myspace photo'.

Getting Intimate

Should you kiss on a first date?

It would be crazy to have rules about this kind of thing, because the only thing that should happen on a first date – or any subsequent date, for that matter – is exactly what the two people on the date want to happen. No more and no less. If you both want to kiss, great. If you don't, that's fine too. How about if one of you wants to kiss and the other doesn't? Well, that brings us to a rule that goes way beyond manners: no one should ever have to do anything intimate that they don't feel one hundred per cent comfortable about doing. It's an important rule. Never forget it.

My mum says that holding hands in public is OK, but kissing in public is rude. I can't see why. What's the story?

Basically, it's rude to make other people feel uncomfortable, and quite a lot of people do feel uncomfortable when they see a couple having a heated snog. Of course, they don't have to look, but that's not the point. I think you can get away with pulling in public if you're somewhere dark (like a club, a quiet street at night or the cinema – but see *Out and About* (p.157) for a few cinema guidelines). It's also OK if you're somewhere semi-private (like a car or under a big tree at a park) where you're not directly in people's view, and they can easily ignore you if they're bothered by it. But you should avoid getting heavy anywhere that is too public.

How do you make the first move?

Making the first move towards physical contact can be really difficult. It's probably best to touch them in a friendly way first (for instance, pick fluff off their hair, touch their arm, etc.). If they flinch away then obviously you won't want to try to become more intimate. But if they seem to like it then try holding hands, and if you want to kiss them, move your head forward slowly (giving them the chance to move away if they don't want to kiss you, saving you both potential embarrassment).

How can you politely brush off a date who's getting too intimate?

If you just want them to cool down, pull away and brightly announce that you fancy doing something else. Try, 'Mmmm. All this exercise has made me hungry! Fancy a snack?' Or, 'I'm getting cramp sitting here! Shall we go for a walk?' A thoughtful date would gladly go along with your wishes. If they're just too overheated to take any notice, you could try making a comment designed to snap them out of the romantic mood, instead. 'I'm dying for a wee!' is good. 'I need to blow my nose,' is even better. 'I think I'm going to be sick!' is more effective still. Seriously, though, if someone is going too far and ignoring your obvious cues to slow down, forget manners. People who won't take no for an answer don't deserve to get treated politely, so if you need to be rude to get them to respect your wishes, do it. Push them off. Swear at them. It's your body and you have a right to defend it any way you want.

Is it rude to lead someone on - to flirt with them if you don't actually want to get intimate?

Let's get this straight: the whole concept of leading someone on is rubbish. Going out on a date or hanging out with someone all night at a party is not a promise to let them snog you – it's a way of getting to know them so that you can make up your mind whether you want to pull them at some point, or not. Snogging someone is not a promise to let them grope you. Letting someone grope you is not a promise to have sex with them. Get the picture? Even if you were actually to say how far you were prepared to go, you'd still have the right to change your mind whenever you wanted. People who accuse others of leading them on are prats. If this happens to you, feel free to forget all about manners and deal with them in any way you like, without feeling guilty.

What if someone takes their date out for a really expensive treat, and gives them a really top time ... Wouldn't it be rude for the date to give them the brush-off after all that?

Oh no. It would be rude – and mad – of the person doing the splashing out to imagine that they have any right to anything at all. You certainly can't buy that right. If you want to take someone on expensive dates, do it because you enjoy it, but don't expect anything in return. If you get taken on an expensive date, never feel that you have to do things you don't want to do.

If you're not sure how far your date is prepared to go, and you accidentally go too far and they get upset, should you apologise?

Sure. It's customary to apologise for accidents of any kind – whether we're talking about accidentally stepping on someone's foot or accidentally assuming that your date would like you to grope them. Once you've said sorry, your date should graciously accept, and the whole thing should be forgotten. But don't forget too well. People are less forgiving the second time you stand on their foot . . .

Your Friends and Your Love Life

If you want to ask someone out whom a friend of yours has already dated, should you check with your friend first, or doesn't it matter once the relationship is finished?

It depends on how the relationship ended. If your friend was dumped, then you should ideally try to forget the whole thing, because your friend might still have feelings for them, and hate the thought of their ex seeing anyone else – let alone a good friend. Even if your mate isn't pining, they might still be so upset about being given the elbow that the thought of you uniting with the enemy will turn them against you too.

Although your friend might not mind so much about your dating people they've finished with, it's common courtesy to take friends' feelings into account, so you should always run it past them. If they tell you that they feel weird about it and would rather you backed off, then you have to decide which is more important to you – your mate's feelings or the date.

When you're getting serious in a relationship, is it rude to see less of your friends? Or is it rude of your friends to expect you to spend less time than you'd like with your partner?

Most people have to face this situation sooner or later, and it's all very much down to how you handle it. It's especially bad behaviour just to dump your loyal mates without giving them any explanation – especially if you have a best friend and the two of you have always been joined at the hip. But if you make an effort to call your friends often, never cancel arrangements you make to see them, and talk to them honestly and openly about your serious new relationship, explaining that it means you'll be seeing less of them for a while, they can't complain. If they act sniffy after you've done your best, then they're the ones being rude and thoughtless.

Is it bad manners to talk to your mates about your dates?

It depends what you say. Put yourself in your date's shoes, and think twice before you repeat anything you wouldn't want passed on if it was about you, such as a personal secret, anything embarrassing that happened, or a word-for-word report on private, nice things that were said. It also depends on why you're spilling – talking about intimate things that happened just for the sake of bragging or gossiping can be a little tacky. But if you're talking about intimate things for a sincere reason to people you trust not to tell anyone else, then that's different, and OK. And finally, it depends on who you say it to. No date could complain about being discussed with your close friends, but they may not be entirely delighted to be greeted with a hearty 'Oooh! I've heard all about you!' from the girl who works in the fish and chip shop that you get a takeaway from once a fortnight.

Your Parents and Your Love Life

When should you introduce a date to your parents?

If any new date comes to pick you up at your home, and your parents are in, it would be rude not to introduce them to each other. And if your parents are super-tense and desperate to know who you're going out with, it's worth keeping them happy with an introduction. This is easily done without much fuss: either get your date to pick you up or walk you home, or get Mum or Dad to drop or collect you when you're going out. If your parents don't mention meeting your dates, then it's up to you. If you've been out on quite a few dates with one person, are getting along very well, and are starting to officially consider them your boyfriend or girlfriend, your parents should get to meet them. They're going to be a big part of your life, and it would be weird not to involve your parents – who are also a big part of your life – in something that is obviously so important to you.

Should you avoid being affectionate with your date or partner in front of your parents, in case it makes them feel uncomfortable?

Well, it all depends on how uptight your parents are, but generally, it should be fine to do innocent, natural things in front of them – like holding hands, putting your arms around each other, looking at each other in an affectionate way or whatever. If they look uncomfortable, though, it's thoughtful to stop whatever you're doing and make a mental note to

21

avoid doing it next time. And if you're wondering whether it's OK to lick each other's ears, pull, remove items of clothing, etc. in front of your parents, then the answer is a resounding no. But you knew that already, right?

Breaking Up

What is the most thoughtful way to break up with someone?

Be totally up-front and honest. It should go without saying that two-timing is cowardly and thoughtless, and so is just letting a relationship tail off without saying anything (e.g. not returning your date's calls, avoiding running into them). Even if you don't care about your date's feelings, you should surely care about your reputation. The best way to finish with someone is to talk face-to-face. It shows courage, respect and good manners.

Writing an email or a letter explaining how you feel is another option, but should only really be used for breaking up relationships that are fairly short-term and not particularly serious. It's pretty insulting and inappropriate to suddenly write an email or letter out of the blue when you've been with someone for months, and have been deeply involved.

Unless you really won't have any chance to see the person face to face, (for instance, if they don't go to your school, socialise with your friends or live anywhere near you), breaking up over the phone isn't really appropriate – it's just way too casual, not to mention cowardly. Breaking up by text or email is never, ever OK. And needless to say, getting someone else to do the dumping for you is probably the suckiest option of all.

Once I've decided how to do the deed, what should I say?

Think and plan carefully before you say anything. The three most important things to do are to be kind, be very clear about what you're trying to say, and – most important of all – give a reason for wanting to break up. If you don't, your boy/girlfriend will be left totally puzzled and freaked out, which is extremely unfair and thoughtless. Your reasons have got to be good, too. Feeding people tacky lines is as cowardly, disrespectful and confusing as giving no reason at all. Don't do it!

Good reasons are ones that make sense. They include:

- Having met someone else you want to go out with.
- Being fed up with a relationship where you always argue.
- Hitting a time in your life when you don't want the stress of going out with anybody (perhaps you've had a personal crisis, or you're coming up for important exams).
- Feeling trapped or scared by a relationship that is getting too serious for you.
- Feeling that your partner treats you badly or thoughtlessly e.g. cheating on you, standing you up, always being late, putting you down, pressuring you into doing things you don't want to do.

Bad reasons are ones that are obscure, meaningless or just a load of clichéd flannel. For instance:

- I need some time alone . . .
- I'm not good enough for you. You deserve better.
- It's just not working out between us . . .
- It's nothing to do with you, there must be something wrong with me . . .

Talking

Conversation

Starting a Conversation

One of the most uncomfortable and nerve-racking situations ever is when you find yourself staring someone in the face – perhaps someone you've just met, or someone you don't know very well – and not knowing what to say. Just the feeling of being stuck for words and that horrible, stony silence can be enough to make you wish the ground would open up and swallow you. And if the person is someone you would like to impress, or would just love to have a chat with, it's even more frustrating. There's no need to panic, though. Even the chattiest people find themselves in spots like this sometimes and, with a little effort, it's not hard to get a conversation going. Here are some tips:

- The best way to start a chat is to ask a question. Choose a question which doesn't have a yes or no answer, so you can get someone talking properly. If you can manage that, you've got the beginnings of a proper conversation, and you're in business.
- Some good subjects to base questions on are:
  - People you both know. If you've been introduced by a mutual friend, you can ask how long they've known one another, or how they met.
  - Things going on around you. If you're at a party, you could ask about what song is playing or who someone else is, even if you know the answer already! You could also pretend that you've just

Talking

arrived, and ask what's happened so far!
- Personal things based on visual clues. If you're beady-eyed, you can almost always find something to ask someone about. If they're holding a carrier-bag with a shop's name on it, you could ask what they bought there. If they're wearing an interesting item of clothing or have an interesting haircut, you could admire it and ask where they got it. If they're wearing a T-shirt or badge with a slogan on it, or have something written on their clothes or bag, you could comment on it and ask what it means. If they've got an injury of some kind, you could ask how it happened. Get the idea?

- Once you've asked your question, listen carefully to the answer. The key to keeping a conversation going is to follow up the things people tell you, by using their answer as a springboard, to carry the conversation on, or take it in another direction. Even if the person hasn't given you much to go on, keep plugging away – ask another question, make a funny comment, anything. Just don't give up. Take this scenario, for example:

> **You (nodding at carrier bag):** What did you buy in WH Smiths?
>
> **Them:** Can't remember. I'm just using the bag to carry stuff.

You could just say, 'Oh', in which case the conversation would have ground to a halt, and you'd be back where you started: with nothing to say. Or you could say, 'Oh well. I think it's a cool bag to carry stuff in. It makes you look very brainy – like you've been buying loads of books or something. Of course, I don't mean that to sound like you're not very brainy . . . I'm sure you are . . . Are you?'

OR:

'You can't remember? God, I wish I could forget all the stuff

I buy in WH Smiths. I spend a fortune in there! I sometimes think that if I stopped shopping there they'd go out of business. I'm a real magazine addict. If I see one I haven't read yet, I just have to get it. Do you read magazines much?'

- After this stage, things get easier, because you've got something to talk about. For instance, if your chat-partner says they do read magazines, you can ask which ones. If there is one that you read too, bingo – you've got loads to talk about. Did they see such and such an article? How long have they been reading it? Do they think it's got better or worse recently? What is their favourite part of the magazine? Even if you don't read any of the same magazines, there's plenty to discuss. You can ask them to tell you about one of their favourite magazines. Or tell them all about one you read that you think they'd like.

- Even if the person's original answer is dismissive, you've started a proper thread of a conversation, and you can keep going with it. Let's say they unhelpfully grunt that they don't read magazines. You can ask what they do read. Books? Which ones? Not books? The back of cereal packets? No? Then what do they do instead of reading? Do they watch a lot of TV? What's their favourite show? Do they spend a lot of time online? Which sites do they like?

That's all there is to it! Happy talking!

Improving Your Chatting Skills

Whether you're with someone you've just met, or your closest friends, it's important to be a good talker. Here are some pointers:

- Everyone has different points of view, so obviously you're not always going to agree with the things people say. Still, you should tread carefully when you disagree with someone. If you act like you think you are right, and they are wrong (even if that's not what you mean), you'll put people's noses out of joint and find your conversations turning into arguments pretty darn pronto. You should always make it clear that your comments are just your opinion, and other people are entitled to have different ones. That way, you can have interesting debates without anyone getting difficult (unless they're too immature to understand that other people are entitled to hold opinions that are different to theirs!).

- The best conversations happen when the people talking feel relaxed and free to say whatever they're thinking. But a side-effect of being laid-back and unguarded like this is that sometimes stupid comments slip out before you have a chance to realise that they're dumb. (Although, of course, some people make dumb comments and never realise it!) It's important not to leap on other people's stupid comments and make fun of them. If you do, they'll feel embarrassed, and that makes the whole atmosphere pretty sour, and can kill the whole conversation stone dead. It will also make people more tense and guarded in the future, which is a shame.

- If you're with a crowd, you should really address everything you say to everyone who is listening. If you've got something to say that would only interest one person, you should either wait until everyone else is stuck in with chats of their own, or fill in the others on the background. Let's say you want to tell one friend some news about another friend whom only the two of you know. Rather than just saying, 'Guess what! Kathy is coming to visit this summer!', it's far nicer to turn to the rest of the crowd and add, 'Our friend Kathy moved to Canada last year and we haven't seen her since!' That way, if anyone else wants to listen in on the rest of the chat about Kathy, they'll know what you're on about. Even if they don't give a stuff, at least you haven't made them feel left out of the conversation – which wouldn't be a nice thing to do.

Listening

The way you listen is just as important – if not more important – than what you say. People who are good listeners are always popular. In fact, some psychology students in the USA once did an experiment to prove it. They all went off separately to spend time chatting with people they'd never met before. Half of the group made an effort to talk lots about very interesting things, make clever conversation and be amusing. The other half deliberately said very little, but listened and acted as if they were very interested in everything that the people they met had to say. Afterwards, the students' teacher interviewed all the people they had met, and asked them to say honestly what they had thought of them. The results were amazing: everyone thought that the listeners were cleverer, friendlier, nicer, more popular and more interesting than the talkers – even though they'd hardly said a word! Here's how to be a good listener:

- Of course, everybody listens, but the important thing is to prove that you're listening. This means nodding and reacting in all the right places, looking all the time at the person who is talking to you (not around the room or over their shoulder), picking up on things that they say (see opposite) and never interrupting.

- Most people are completely useless when it comes to listening to other people tell funny or interesting true stories. What you should do is listen to the anecdote, maybe drop in the odd reaction along the way ('Really?', 'What happened next?', 'What did she say?', etc.) and, when it's finished, prove that you listened, understood and appreciated it in whatever way it was intended. In other words, laugh if it's funny, gasp if it's shocking, say, 'I'd love to have been there!' or 'How weird!' or just, 'That's a great story!' – whatever. For some strange reason, though, as someone else starts telling an anecdote, everyone else gets overtaken by a burning urge to talk about themselves. How many times have you said: 'You know, the same thing happened to me!' or 'Funny you should say that, because . . '. or 'That reminds me . . .'? You should never say any of the above during someone else's anecdote, and only say them afterwards if you've reacted to their story first. It takes a bit of effort and concentration, but it's wildly important.

Questions

Questions are a brilliant invention – they get conversations moving, they help you learn things, they stop you from feeling confused. However, questions can also get you into trouble, by offending people. Unless you're talking to a close friend or your parents, you should handle questions with care. Here's how.

- Don't ask questions about money, like, 'Are you rich?', 'How much do you get paid?' or 'How much did that cost?' (whether you're talking about anything from a pair of shoes to a house). You shouldn't really even ask if something was expensive. Why not? Because other people's finances are none of your business!

- Avoid asking people you don't know well about very personal subjects. This would include anything about their relationships or sex lives (e.g. 'Are you a virgin?' or 'Are you gay?').

- If you're interested in someone's political opinions, it's fine to ask what they think about specific subjects, but you shouldn't ask directly which party they vote for (or would vote for) – some people don't like to say.

- Don't ask questions about someone's appearance unless you know them very well. For instance, you shouldn't ask someone with a birthmark 'What's that?', or ask someone with big feet what shoe size they wear – it could make them feel very self-conscious. Weight is another issue that's always best avoided, especially if someone is on the chunky or skinny side.

- When you're talking to someone with a disability, you don't need to ignore their disability totally, but you should avoid asking questions that are stupid. For instance, it would be fine to ask a blind person about their guide dog, or ask if they can read braille (which is just making friendly conversation), but it would be stupid to ask them 'What's it like being blind, then?' or ask someone in a wheelchair 'What happened to you?'. You should never ask personal questions either (like, 'Can you have sex?') unless you are very close friends. Even if your questions are intelligent, don't ask too many of them – people with disabilities generally find it very boring to discuss their disabilities endlessly, and would rather chat about all the same subjects that anyone else would.

- If you've asked someone a question that they seem reluctant to answer, drop the subject – don't keep plugging away, even if you can't understand why they wouldn't want to talk about it.

Have You Heard the One About . . .?

You wouldn't think that something as simple as telling a joke could have its pitfalls, but it does. Here they are:
- If someone starts to tell a joke and you know it, it's polite

to keep quiet and hear it out. Cutting in with cries of 'I know this!', or groans of 'Heard it . . .' is mean, and saying the punchline yourself is even meaner – especially if you say it first and get the laugh. The only time it's OK to stop someone who's started telling a joke you've heard is if it's one of those vile, endless shaggy dog stories which go on forever and aren't even funny. Anyone who would subject you to one of those (especially one you've already heard) doesn't deserve any special treatment!

- You should always force a laugh at other people's jokes, even if you've heard them already or they're just crushingly unfunny. Why? Because nothing makes a person feel more silly and uneasy than cracking a joke and being greeted with a stony silence.

- The only exception to the above would be if the joke was bad taste. Then you could either ignore it, or say, 'I hate jokes like that', and change the subject.

- Because it's embarrassing to explain a joke, you shouldn't put anyone else in a position where they have to do it. If you don't get a joke, it's best to laugh anyway and ask someone else to explain it later. Don't overdo it though – as the old saying goes, he who laughs loudest doesn't understand the joke!

- If you're halfway through a bad–taste joke and you can see that someone is getting upset, it's always better to stop dead and say something like 'Actually I can see that this isn't your kind of thing . . . Forget it'. If you say it in a tone that is friendly (with not a trace of grumpiness or snottiness), and change the subject quickly afterwards, it shouldn't turn out to be too embarrassing a situation.

- If you realise that you've messed up a joke, or forgotten the punchline, it's best to own up and drop the whole thing as quickly as possible. If you dither around and try to struggle through it, it's embarrassing for you and for everyone else who has to patiently listen to your ramblings and pretend to laugh afterwards.

Don't Tell Anyone I Told You This, But . . .

After snogging, gossiping is just about the most fun you can have with your mouth open. But if you want to be popular and well thought of (and who doesn't?) you've got to play it safe.

- Peppering your chat with delicious titbits of scandal can be tempting because, all of a sudden, everyone is all ears and hanging on to your every word. But don't be fooled into thinking that this makes you more popular. In fact, it can give people a lower opinion of you. Basically, most people are ridiculously hypocritical; they love to hear gossip, and hate to be gossiped about. So while they're happily lapping up everything a gossip has to say, they're also making mental notes not to trust them in the future. Gossiping can make people interested in you, and scared of you, but it won't make them like you. So if you want to be well-liked, gossip only to your closest friends – and never gossip about them!

- The only thing people like to hear more than gossip is gossip that they're really not supposed to hear. Unlike gossip, though, which is fine in certain circumstances, I can't think of a single situation where it's excusable to pass on something that you've been sworn to silence over. If you do it, you've got to be prepared to face the consequences. And the consequences usually consist of the person who told you the secret flying off the handle (which, luckily, is usually temporary) and totally losing their trust in you (which, sadly, is usually permanent). Don't bother making excuses – all you can do is apologise and swear you'll never do it again. And don't even bother getting embroiled in a row with the person who you told the secret to who swore they wouldn't tell the person whose secret it was in the first place. Sure, they betrayed your trust, but why should you expect people to keep their traps shut for you if you can't keep yours shut for anyone else? However hurt and annoyed you are by them, you can bet that the person you betrayed feels a squillion times worse.

Now What Do I Say?

There are certain times when even champion chatterboxes aren't sure what to say next. It pays to figure out which situations are the ones that throw you, so you can plan your tactics ahead. Here are some common problems:

What should you do if you accidentally say something you shouldn't have? Should you apologise?

The best thing to do when you realise you've put your foot in it is to smile and say something like, 'I'm sorry! That didn't come out sounding quite the way I meant it!', and then carry on quickly as if nothing had happened. If you start going into detail about what you said, and trying to go back on it, you're likely to get into even deeper water.

I never know what to say when people act like they feel sorry for me. Any tips?

The best thing to say is just, 'Thank you', or maybe 'I appreciate you saying that'. It can be horrible if you feel that someone is actually pitying you, but remember that when people are being sympathetic, they're usually just trying to be nice, and are probably feeling as awkward as you are. Because of this, it makes more sense to simply change the subject than ask, 'What exactly do you mean?' or get annoyed and say 'You don't need to feel sorry for me' – which could embarrass them.

What should you say when someone pays you a compliment?

Say thank you. You don't need to say anything else, especially if the compliment is about something you're wearing or something you own, rather than actually about you or something you've done. If you feel that you must say something else, try, 'It's very kind of you to say so', or, 'You've made my day!', and then change the subject. It's boring, and a waste of time to come over all coy ('Ooh, stop it!', 'Do you really think so?', 'Really?', 'No, you're just saying that . . .' etc.), and it's rude and dismissive to disagree ('Whaaat??? You're kidding?', 'No way! You must be mad!'). And you don't need to pay someone a compliment back when they've complimented you. So just say thanks. That's it.

What's a backhanded compliment?

It's a comment which sounds like a compliment, but is insulting at the same time. There's an old joke about them – I can't remember it exactly, but the punchline is 'You sweat less than any fat girl I know'. Of course, no one would ever say anything that foul and stupid to someone (I hope), but you get the general idea. Sometimes backhanded compliments just slip out by accident, but you should try not to let that happen to you. As a general guideline, avoid comments like, 'It's very good considering . . .'. or describe something in a lukewarm way (e.g. 'Not bad', 'A really good effort', 'OK') – it's better to say nothing at all!

Complaining

Everybody has times when they're less than happy about something they've bought, how they've been treated, or any number of other things. People used to think it was good manners never to complain about anything – a tradition which makes no sense at all. Complaining isn't rude, as long as you're complaining for a purpose (e.g. to ask for the situation to be set right, to help improve things in the future, whatever) and as long as you don't fly off the handle at someone who isn't at fault. Here are a few common situations, and how to handle them:

You bought something and discovered that it was damaged when you got home.

Take it back to the place you bought it and explain cheerfully that you are certain that the damage was already done, you have not used or worn it, and you would like a replacement, credit note or refund. If the sales person refuses to believe you, ask politely to see the manager and tell him or her the same thing. If you get the same reaction, it can be worth giving up temporarily, and coming back with an adult. Pathetically, you might find that the same people who gave you a horrendous time will grovel to an adult – especially an adult who threatens not to shop with them again.

Something you've bought has broken or fallen apart.

Take it back as soon as possible and explain that you were only using the item for the purpose for which it was intended and don't think it should have fallen to bits so soon. Ask for a replacement, credit note or refund. If you have no joy, ask for the manager and go through it all again. Still no luck? Don't get in a temper; the shop may not have actually made the item. Ask nicely for a phone number or address of the manufacturers. You are entitled to this. Once you've got it, ring or write to them instead.

You've just had your hair done and you hate it.

If the disaster was your fault (e.g. you got the haircut you asked for and found that it didn't suit you, or you asked them to do whatever they wanted and then decided you didn't like it) there's not much you can do. Otherwise, you should be able to get the mess put right, free of charge, as long as you speak up right away. If you force a smile and pay up, then come back to whinge later when you've mustered some courage (and had time to get really upset), you'll probably be sent on your way. So what do you say? You're most likely to get a result if you're calm. Seeing as you probably want to strangle the idiot who butchered your hair, you'll be calmer speaking to the manager instead. Explain that you're not at all happy with the cut and you would like someone else in the salon to give you another haircut/colour job to put it right. Add that you explained quite clearly what you wanted and the stylist didn't pay any attention, therefore you don't feel that you should have to pay for the second session.

You're eating out and the person serving you is very rude.

Don't bother grousing to them directly – it'll cause a scene and won't solve anything. The best way of making your feelings known is to leave only a small tip, or not to leave one at all (see *Tipping* – p.166). However, you should also tell the manager why you haven't left a tip – that way they can set about adjusting their employee's attitude problem.

You're eating out and the food takes ages to arrive.

Complain to the person serving you, but do it politely and calmly – it's almost certainly not their fault, but the fault of the people cooking the food. No luck? Take your complaint to the manager.

You worked really hard on something at school or college and got a lousy mark.

Get your teacher alone and explain why you don't feel their marking was fair. Then explain why you mentioned it – perhaps you just wanted to make your feelings known, or maybe you actually wanted something: a simple explanation for the bad mark, someone to re-read and re-mark the work or the chance to do it again. If you explain well, the teacher shouldn't get difficult.

You worked hard at a job and got paid or tipped very badly.

Put on a friendly face and ask, 'Excuse me, but was there

something wrong with my work?'. Explain that you only asked because you usually get paid or tipped more, and therefore you assumed that maybe there was something wrong. If you can manage to say all this in a cheerfully innocent tone, you should get an explanation at the very least, or – better still – a bit more money. Of course, if there was something wrong with your work, you're probably onto a loser, although it's worth having a shot at looking very sad and saying, 'Well, I did my best . . .' in a feeble voice.

Communicating

Letters

People have been writing letters to one another for years, so it's not really surprising that there are so many rules and traditions about communicating by post. Some are old-fashioned and outdated, but others are still pretty useful. Some general points to remember:

- Letters are private. And we're not just talking manners here, it's the law: it's illegal to open a letter that's not addressed to you.

- Bearing in mind that letters are private, you shouldn't really show a letter around to other people. If you're desperate to do it, use your good judgement. A friend who has written a chatty letter about what he's been up to on his long summer trip away probably wouldn't mind if you showed it to a mutual friend who was keen to hear his news. However, anyone who had written you a romantic letter with a soppy poem in it would probably be upset at the very thought of someone else reading it. (This rule also applies to email, of course!)

- Postcards are much less private than letters. This means that it's fine to show postcards you've received to other people, if they want to see them. It also means that you should be careful what you say on them: your best mate probably won't be too delighted with you if you write, *Weather's great. Wish you were here. Hope you're well and that your brother hasn't discovered the big stain on that jacket of his that you borrowed last week.*

- It's not just what you say in a letter that counts. Bad

spelling, loads of crossing out, repeating yourself and using ripped up scraps of school book paper all give the distinct impression that you couldn't be bothered to write in the first place. If you send this kind of letter, you should at least say sorry and give a reason e.g. you were madly busy).

- When you want people to take you seriously, you should always send a neat letter, on plain white or cream paper, preferably word-processed, with as few mistakes as possible. Save the cute notepaper and handwritten letters for friends, relatives, pen-pals and fan-mail.

- If you just want to say *Thank you, Congratulations, Good luck* or *Get well soon*, but you don't want to write a long letter, sending a greetings card is fine. However, you should always write your own message on the card, not just the person's name and your name, or it's really boring and impersonal, and makes you look lazy and/or brain-dead.

- If you're writing more than one page, it's a good idea to start your second page on a fresh sheet of paper, rather than write on the back of the first one. This is because the writing could show through on both sides and make your letter hard to read, depending on the kind of paper you use.

- When you've got a letter that's more than one page long, you can write PTO at the bottom of each page that has another page following it, if you want. This stands for Please Turn Over, and lets the person reading it know that there's more to come. If you're writing on both sides of a sheet of paper, you should definitely use it. It helps to number your pages as well.

- PS stands for Postscript, which means an afterthought – something you decided that you wanted to add after you'd already signed the letter. If you want to add another PS, you're supposed to mark it PPS. A third would be PPPS, and so on. All this is fine for casual letters, but doesn't work on formal letters, so if you're trying to look organised, plan your letter before you write it so you won't need to use postscripts.

It doesn't really matter how you lay out letters to friends, pen-pals, relatives, etc. but in formal letters like the ones you might send to your bank, or to a newspaper, or to an MP, the layout is very important. Here's how a formal letter should look:

Your name
Your address
Your phone number/mobile number
Your email address

Name of person you're writing to
Their job title and company name (if necessary)
Their address

The date

Dear So-and-so,

Blah blah blah blah blah. Blah blah blah blah blah. Blah blah blah blah blah. Blah blah blah blah blah blah. Blah blah blah blah.

Sign off,

Your name.

Let's take a more detailed look at all the different bits . . .

Names and Addresses

• Write each piece of information on a new line. For example:

Mr Stuart Jones,
The Manager,
Greenstuff Bank,
Chudley Station Branch,
32 Station Road,
Chudley-Under-Bucket,
Twiddlesborough TW5 4NQ

- On a less formal letter, you can leave off the name and address of the person you're writing to.
- Needless to say, if you've got writing paper with your address printed on it, you don't need to write it as well! If you don't, you can write your name and contact details in the top centre of the page, or to the right-hand side.
- If you're writing to someone in another country, add the country you live in at the bottom of your address.
- People usually write their phone numbers like this:
  Telephone: (0167) 862 2295
  with the word Telephone or Tel first, followed by a colon (:), and the area code in brackets.

The Dear So-and-So Bit

- If you're writing to a friend or relative, you'd obviously call them by their name, nickname or whatever other name you fancy.
- If you're writing a sensible letter to an adult you don't know, or don't know very well, you should call them Mr So-and-so, or Ms So-and-so, even if you know their first name. The exceptions would be a) if you didn't know their surname, and b) if you were replying to a letter from them, and they had signed the letter using their first name.
- When you're writing to a woman, you're safest using the title Ms, which is used for married women and unmarried women. But if you were writing to a woman whom you

44

knew for sure called herself Mrs or Miss, you could use that instead.

- Similarly, if you know that someone uses a different title – e.g. Dr, Professor, Lady – you should use it.
- You should always use either a first name, or a title and a last name. In other words, you shouldn't really write *Dear Mr Stuart Jones* or *Dear Stuart Jones* – only *Dear Stuart*, or *Dear Mr Jones* (but having said that, plenty of people do).
- If you're writing a very sensible letter to someone you reckon is very important, you can write *Dear Sir* or *Dear Madam* instead of their name.
- When you don't know the name of the person you're writing to – say you were writing to the manager of a big company, a shop or a department of the local council – you'd write *Dear Sirs* (pretty sexist, huh?), *Dear Sir or Madam* or *To whom it may concern*. Of course, you could always telephone first, and ask who your letter should be sent to – then you'd have a name to use instead.

The Sign-off bit

How you sign off depends on what you wrote in the dear so-and-so bit. Again, if you're writing to a friend or relative, write whatever you fancy.

If you used the person's first name, you've got a pretty wide choice of ways to sign off. Friendly terms include *Love*, *Best wishes*, *All the best* and *Regards* and *Kind regards*. If you want to sound more formal, you can say *Yours truly*, *Yours sincerely* or just *Sincerely*.

When you're writing a business letter or any other kind of serious letter, you should never sign off with *Love*, even if you've used the person's first name.

If you used the person's title and last name, you're supposed to always sign off *Yours sincerely*. However, if you're friendly with the person and just used their last name as a mark of respect (let's say it was a letter to a teacher you get on well with), you can go for something less stuffy like *Best wishes*, *All the best* and *Regards*.

If you're not using their name, i.e. you used *Dear Sir* or something similar, you should always use *Yours faithfully* to sign off.

Your Signature

- In formal, printed letters, you're supposed to write your name, leaving a big enough gap above it to sign your name, like this:

Yours sincerely,

Ella Robinson

Miss Ella Robinson

- You don't have to do this in other letters, or in letters that are handwritten, but if your signature is hard to read, it's not a bad idea to do it anyway.
- As long as you've written your full title, you can sign however you want. For a formal letter, scribble either your full name (but not your title) or your initial and last name. For a less stuffy letter you can use just your first name.
- If you're one of those people with a wacky signature (such as a cute little happy face instead of a dot over the letter i, or little stars and squiggles bursting around the whole thing), it's probably best to develop a sensible, boring version to use for sensible, boring letters.

Everything You Need to Know About Addressing Envelopes

- The address should go in the centre of the envelope, or slightly to the left. This is so that there is room for the post-mark to go over the stamp without blotting out any of the address. Some people indent each new line.
- Be sure to use the right title (Mr, Ms, etc.) for the person you're writing to (see *The dear-so-and-so* bit, p.44).
- Put each piece of info on a separate line.
- Write really clearly.
- Don't forget the postcode!
- It's a good idea to write your address on the envelope so that it can be returned if it gets lost. To avoid any confusion you should write *From:* before the address (and your name, if you want), and do the whole thing on the front left-hand corner or back of the envelope, in small writing.

Thank-you Letters

When do you have to write a thank-you letter for a present?

Thank-you letters and thank-you cards are for saying thank you when you didn't get a chance to do it personally. So if someone sends you a gift in the post, or gives it to someone else to give to you, a thank-you letter or card is in order. The same is true if someone gives you a gift themselves, but you don't open it until later, when they're not around. Bear this in mind if you're the type who likes saving all their Christmas or birthday pressies to open on the big day itself, or you prefer to wait until your birthday party is over before opening the things people have bought. Either of these habits will leave you with plenty of scribbling to do.

So you never have to write if you've already said thanks?

Well, every rule has its exceptions. It's also nice to write if:

- You may have been a bit dismissive when you said thanks (e.g. you were at your party and in a rush to get back to socialising).
- The present was surprisingly extravagant or expensive.
- The present was home-made, or had obviously had a lot of time and effort put into it in some other way (say someone had queued up for ages to get you tickets to see your favourite band).
- The present was money (it's nice to let the person who gave it to you know what you spent it on, or what you plan to do with it).

What makes a good thank-you letter?

What you write isn't as important as when you write. Ideally, your letter or card should be in the post soon after you open the present – you shouldn't wait longer than a week to get writing.

What should you write? You can't go too far wrong if you follow these simple guidelines:

- Say right away that you're writing to say thank you.
- Mention what the present was (don't just say thanks for the present).
- Say how much you liked it, and put in a personal comment (e.g. *I wore it the other day and everyone said how nice it was or I've started reading it already and I'm hooked!*).
- Don't forget that it's rude to mention money, even if you're just trying to say something nice (e.g. *It must have cost a lot!*).
- Never say anything negative (e.g. *It's not the sort of thing I*

usually like, but . . . , Someone else gave me the same thing! or *Sadly it's broken already!*).

- If the present was money or a voucher, say what you plan to buy. If you don't know, invent something or say you're saving it.

Do you have to write thank-you letters for favours or other things that people do for you?

You should always write and thank someone who has had you to stay with them for any length of time or overnight if it's someone you don't know very well. You should tell them how much you enjoyed it, and also thank them for any specific, nice things they did while you were staying – like taking you out for a meal or an outing or buying you something.

You don't have to write to thank people for favours. However, if you've borrowed something and the person who lent it to you is not around when you give it back (perhaps you've given it to someone else to pass on to them, or dropped it round while they're out), you should always stick a little thank-you note in with it.

If you don't want to write a thank-you card or letter, will an email, text or phonecall do?

Sure. These days giving someone a call, sending a text or dropping them an email to say thanks, instead of writing, is absolutely fine. Having said that, old people often prefer to get the more traditional letter or card (even if they use email) but a call, text or email is certainly better than nothing!

In terms of what you write, a thank-you email or text should follow all the same guidelines for a thank-you letter (see p.47). A thank-you call should be just as personal and specific. In other words, you should say you're calling to thank them for the lovely present right away, before you talk about anything else, and you should also follow the general guidelines. Once you've done the thank-you thing, it's fine to have a chat if you want, and equally OK to keep the conversation short if you only wanted to say thank you.

Do you have to reply to thank-you letters that people send you?

No, people don't expect answers to thank-you letters. But if the thank-you bit is followed by lots of chatty information, or questions, then it counts as a regular letter, and it would be rude not to get in touch with the person who wrote it soon, either by letter or phone.

The Phone

Whether or not you're one of those people who seem to have their mobile permanently glued to their ear, there are a few tips about using the phone that everyone should know if they want to get ahead in life. Let's check them out:

THE TEN COMMANDMENTS OF USING THE PHONE.

1. Thou shalt answer the landline nicely

The best way to answer is saying 'Hello?' When a call is for someone else, ask 'Who is it please?' or 'Who shall I say is calling?', then either hand over the phone (if the person is in the room) or go and get them, telling them who is on the phone. If you're too lazy to go and get them and you'd rather yell, cover the mouthpiece or move away from the phone first, or the poor person on the other end will get deafened by your bellowing! It's also nice manners to go back to the phone and tell the caller that the person they called for is just coming, and will be with them in a moment.

2. Thou shalt identify thyself, pronto

Since the days of mobiles, we've all got so used to people seeing our names on their screens and knowing it's us calling them, that it's easy to forget to identify yourself when you're calling a landline number, or someone who doesn't have your number stored. Saying who you are right away is a good habit to get into, even when calling mobile to mobile – it's helpful and polite and it saves people having to ask who they're talking to if, for whatever reason, they don't know.

If you're calling a landline and you know the person who has answered the phone, you should always say who you are and maybe ask how they're doing, even if you've called to speak to someone else.

3. Thou shalt check that the person thou is calling is able to talk before launching into a long rant

Your calls will always be welcome if you take a second to ask if you've called at a good time – before you start rambling.

4. Thou shalt give thy phone conversation full attention

There's nothing more irritating than someone who goes 'Mmm' in all the wrong places, has long, mysterious silences or suddenly shouts things like, 'What is she wearing?!!!!', 'Hooray, I've found the magic dinosaur egg!' or 'Go away you little pest!'. If you're utterly desperate to read a magazine, watch telly, play a video game or insult members of your family, do everyone a favour and put off the phonecall until later, when you're not going to be distracted.

5. If thou hast to talk to someone in the room while thou is on the phone, thou shalt say 'Excuse me . . .' or 'Hold, on a minute . . .' first

Otherwise it gets confusing. However, if there's someone in the room whom you're actually supposed to be spending time with, you should really explain to the person on the phone that you can't talk now, and call them back later instead.

6. Thou shalt not make any gross noises

Any noise you make near the phone comes out crisply and directly into the ear of the person you're talking to. This is why you should avoid eating, drinking, chewing gum and blowing your nose while you're on the phone – nobody wants a hundred decibels worth of your chomping, slurping or nose noises broadcast directly into their ear, thank you.

7. Thou shalt always apologise when thou gets a wrong number

Even if you realise right away (e.g. some doddery old woman answers when you were trying to get Dial-a-pizza), you should never just slam the phone down.

8. Thou shalt respect the poor person who pays the bill

This means that when using your home landline, or – unless you use pay-as-you-go – your mobile, you should always check with whoever pays the bill before calling long-distance, mobile numbers or any other number charged at more than the standard rate (like TV phone votes, most competitions advertised in magazines and on TV and anything else advertised as premium rate). This also means asking permission before you get new ringtones and other downloads for your mobile, and not making long, chatty, personal calls from other people's landlines and mobiles.

9. Thou shalt be really cool about giving and taking messages

If you answer a call for someone who's not around, you should always offer to take a message, jot the details down and make sure the other person gets it. If you call someone's land-line and they're not around, you should always ask the person who answers if they mind taking a message, and make it brief and clear.

10. Thou shalt be thoughtful to other landline users

This means keeping calls short when other people want to use the phone. It also means not making or taking calls too late at night or early in the morning when you might wake people up. And you should also tread carefully with the jokey stuff. For instance, don't ring a friend and say 'Hello Stinky!' in a funny voice unless you're certain it's them on the line (their dad might not appreciate the joke quite as much). Similarly, don't answer your home phone saying, 'Hello! The nut house! Can I help you?' when you're expecting a call from a friend – it might not be them!

If you don't have a mobile, or you do, but you don't have any signal/battery/credit, are there any rules about using other people's mobiles or landlines?

You bet. Here they are:
- Never use anybody's phone without asking first.
- When you ask to use someone's phone, it's polite to always say who it is that you want to call, and why.
- You should really only borrow someone's phone to call your parents – for instance to make an arrangement, to let them know about a change of plans, or to say that you've arrived somewhere safely.

- You should only call other people if it's to say something important and specific. It would be fine, for instance, to check up on someone who was ill, make an arrangement or wish a friend happy birthday. But you should always explain upfront that you're on someone else's phone, get to the point right away and not chat for hours afterwards.
- Always keep calls brief, especially if they're to a mobile or long-distance number.
- If you've used the landline a lot while you've been staying with someone, or have made a long call on a friend's mobile, it's polite to offer to pay some money towards the bill. The chances are that your offer will be refused, but it's a nice gesture to make anyway.
- You should never answer someone else's phone unless they ask you to.

Nettiquette

The internet is just about the most fun tool for communication ever invented. Not only has it revived the tradition of using the written word to keep in touch with friends, but it's also allowed people to spread their social nets wider than ever before – making brand new friends and staying in touch with old ones regardless of where they live, go to school or hang out.

However you communicate online, the most important thing to remember, above all else, is safety. You should never give out personal information like your full name, the name of your school, your address or any other information that could allow someone to find out exactly who and where you are. And always remember that people aren't necessarily who, what or how old they say they are. If someone you've met online asks to meet you in real life, you shouldn't even consider agreeing until you've discussed it with your parents.

Once you've got your safety precautions straight, though, the online world is your oyster. However you use the internet to communicate, here are a few basics that everyone should know:

- Never write all in capitals – it's hard on the eye and looks like you're shouting!

- Always remember that when you're communicating with the written word, you need to make sure that your tone is clear. When someone is talking, it's easy to tell whether they're being playful, teasing or sarcastic. But the same words in writing can come across very differently. Whether you use emoticons (e.g. smiley faces, or winky, frowny or shocked ones!), strike-through text or just extra words (e.g. *only kidding!*), always make sure that someone else will understand what you said, in the exact way you meant it to sound, and won't misinterpret you and possibly get upset.

- Almost everybody is bolder on the internet than they are in real life. With a computer screen safely between you and the world, and plenty of time to think of the perfect thing to say, it's very easy to end up being flirtier, tougher, and more confident than you are in person. This can be a good thing, but it can also get you into all sorts of trouble. Before you write anything – especially a flirty comment or a rude put-down, always ask yourself if you would say it to the person's face. If you wouldn't, think twice before you type.

Social Networking Sites

Networking sites such as Myspace, where you have a personal page and add friends, are great fun and can be very addictive! My best tip is to make sure that your real social life doesn't suffer because you spend so much time on your virtual social life! But the following hints should help you get the most out of your online social network, stay popular and avoid upset.

- You should never use the same display nickname or personal quote as anyone else. Names and quotes are part of people's online identities, and although someone may be flattered that you liked something of theirs enough to copy it, they're more likely to be annoyed – it's a bit like copying someone's exact clothes and hairstyle. Even if they change to a new a name or quote, it doesn't mean that the old one is up for grabs – they may want to go back to it sometime. If you feel you have every right to use a name or quote – say, if it's a well-known comedy catchphrase or a lyric from a song – it's still good manners to ask the person who used it first whether they mind.

- Layout designs are equally personal, and you should never steal a layout design code, or choose a layout design from a layout site that you've seen on a page belonging to anyone you know.

- People can also get upset if others put the same song or video as them on their homepage, but I think this is a little over-sensitive! If it's something obscure that you've only ever seen on their page, you should think twice, but if it's a popular song or clip, they don't really have any right to get angry. Either way, though, it's thoughtful to send a little mail letting someone know you're adding something that they had first, and saying that you hope they don't mind.

- Beware of joining train schemes that promise to extend your friend network. They work by sending out automated bulletins to your friends suggesting that they add you, but by joining up, you are also effectively signing your friends up to receive hundreds of bulletins about other people on the scheme and often other spam mail as well. These schemes clog up people's bulletin boxes, and can make you very unpopular – avoid them!

- If you send someone a friend request and they turn you down, you should leave it at that. Sending a second request is pestering, and sending a mail asking why they turned you down is even worse. People turn down friend requests for all kinds of reasons, and it's important to respect their right to do it. Though, of course, if the person who turned you down is someone you're friends with in real life and you think they must have made a mistake, that's different.

- If you're sending a friend request to someone you don't know in real life, it's nice to send them a little mail at the same time, explaining who you are or why you wanted to add them. It doesn't have to be long or complicated – *I know your mate Emma* or *You don't know me, but I like your taste in music* or *You have cool hair!* are perfectly acceptable reasons to give!

- If someone you don't know sends you a friend request but doesn't send a message, it's fine to send them a quick mail asking who they are before you decide whether to accept or not.

- If someone accepts your friend request – especially a friend-of-a-friend or someone you don't know in real life, always post a comment on their board to say thanks for the add.

- It's considered bad form to complain to someone if you are not in their 'top friends' box, even if you feel you should be. But at the same time, it's important to keep people's feelings in mind. If someone is a close friend in real life, you should really have them up there – not just people who look cool! If someone has you in their top eight, you should consider returning the honour – although obviously not if you hardly know them or can't understand why they've put you in there!

- If someone leaves you a picture comment, it's the done thing to return the favour, or thank them for it, or ideally both!
- Comments boards are a weird thing – they're essentially public, because everybody can read everybody else's (and lots of people do!), but despite this, they're considered private. It's considered dodgy behaviour to comment on anything you've read on someone else's comment board – it's a bit like eavesdropping. Look at it this way – even if a real-life private conversation is taking place within earshot, it doesn't automatically mean that you're invited to join in.
- Don't delete comments from your board – it's hurtful to the person who posted the comment as it looks like you're embarrassed to be seen talking to them! The exceptions to this rule would be if the comment was abusive (in which case you should not only delete it, but also block the person who sent it!) or if the comment contained something that you wouldn't want others visiting your page to see – like a secret or a mean comment about someone else. Needless to say, no one should post comments like that in the first place – they belong in private mail.
- Don't clog people's bulletin boards! A lot of people misuse bulletins, and although some people don't mind, and just ignore the mountains of trash in their bulletin box, others get really annoyed. In order to avoid irritating people, anything directed to just one person, or that would interest only a few of your friends, should go on a comment board or in a personal mail. Musings on how you're feeling or what happened at the weekend belong in your blog. And a cut-and-paste of the hilarious conversation you and your best friend had on MSN last night doesn't really belong anywhere, but especially not in a bulletin! If you really can't restrain yourself from sharing your every thought with several hundred people, at least make sure you make

the heading clear and relevant: e.g. *OMG! I just got a new puppy!* or *OMG! Just saw that funny advert for yogurt!* is a more useful heading than just *OMG!*. That way, people who are close enough to you that they want to hear your opinion on the yogurt advert just as much as news of a new puppy can do so, and those that aren't don't have to!

- Bulletins are essentially group mails, so it's worth checking out p.65 for some more useful guidelines on what to send and what not to send.

Forums, Chat-boards and Groups

Whether you're looking for an answer to a question or are just keen to discuss your favourite TV show or music with like-minded people across the world, boards and groups are a great place to be. But they can also be pretty daunting – your first time posting to a new group can be a bit like walking into a room full of strangers who all know each other and are in the middle of a conversation! But there are definitely measures you can take to make sure that you'll fit in and be warmly welcomed. Here are some tips:

- Most importantly, always lurk before you post. In other words, read what everyone else is saying and get a feel for the community before you join in. Some people lurk for weeks before their first post, so don't feel that you're being silly if you feel more comfortable waiting and reading for a while.
- Try to figure out what's appropriate to discuss – some fan groups only like to discuss their hero's work and don't like talking about that person's private life, while on other groups, you can be as gossipy as you like!
- As well as getting a feel for the kind of things that are cool to talk about, check out the style used in the postings and

fall in with it. Some groups are fine with txt abbreviations, l33t-speak and swearing, others aren't.

- Don't troll! Trolling is different to simply expressing a negative opinion. As long as you don't mind kicking off a heated discussion, it's fine, for instance, to post to a TV show's fan board with a comment like *The new series isn't as good as the last one*. But saying *This show is rubbish! You're all mad!* is trolling. If you come across a board discussing something or someone you don't like, just leave!

- Don't feed the troll! Trolling is a waste of everybody's time, and most boards and groups get rid of trolls by ignoring them. It can be tempting to answer back when someone is slating something or someone you like, but it'll only encourage the troll to stay around and argue, and the rest of the group won't thank you for that.

- Flaming – getting into a war of words with someone – is part of life online, and some people actively enjoy it! But it's important to keep flame wars under control and know when it's time to agree to disagree. If you keep disputes going endlessly, it takes up a lot of space and gets very boring for everybody else. If you really can't stop fighting after a few exchanges, it's thoughtful to move the dispute off the board and into email or Instant Message.

- Be careful of going off topic. Stick to posts that discuss things which are directly related to the subject. If you're not sure whether something you want to discuss is off-topic or not (e.g. if you're on a TV show fan board and you want to discuss a different show that the lead actor was in), always put *OT:* before the description in your subject line.

- Long posts that include copies of more than one previous post (double quoting) can take up a lot of space and be annoying to read. If you must quote, only use the most recent post in the thread, and always trim it to include only the relevant bit, not the entire thing.

- Think carefully before you post anything other than words – a lot of groups frown on pictures, html, sound files or even elaborate signature files! Look at what everyone else is doing, and if in any doubt, don't post it. If you have something special that you think everyone would love to see or hear, post a link, instead. Or, if it's something only you have and you have a personal page, you could upload it there and post to let people know that it's there if they want to see it.

- Always do your research before posting large files – even to groups that regularly share pictures, video clips and creative writing, such as Livejournal communities. Livejournal users, for instance, often prefer to use an LJ cut – a simple system where you describe the contents of the post and provide a clickable link to it, so that people can choose whether to view the file or not. Failing to do this takes up space and loading time, and can be considered very bad form!

- If you've come to a group for the first time looking for the answer to a question, always make sure it hasn't been answered already. Don't ask anything until you've read all the existing threads. Long-established groups may also have a FAQ list where you might be able to find the info you're looking for – always read it before you waste other people's time by asking a frequently asked question!

- When you're stuck on a particularly tricky piece of home-work, especially at exam level, it can be tempting to post a question on a specialist message board in search of an answer. People on specialist groups are generally not very keen on this! If you really cannot find the answer you're looking for anywhere else and are determined to go ahead, remind yourself that you are essentially approaching a group of strangers who are in the middle of a conversation and asking them for help! Don't just post your question –

always introduce yourself, explain your situation, say please and tell the group how grateful you would be if someone would come to your aid!

- When discussing movies, books and TV shows, be very, very careful of spoilers. Never write anything like *I can't believe he dies at the end!* and don't assume that everyone has seen or read everything that you have, even if you're on a specific group for a book, show or movie. Ruining a surprise – or even just a minor plot point – will get you into huge trouble. If you think your post might contain a spoiler, always put a spoiler warning in your subject line. It's also nice to include spoiler space within the post – another spoiler warning followed by several blank lines so that people have to make an active decision to scroll down to read what you've written, rather than stumbling on it accidentally.

- Many boards and forums use avatars or icons – little pictures that represent the individuals posting on the board. As much as you might admire someone else's you should never use the same one without permission. Bear in mind that many people make their own icons, so you may actually be stealing, not just copying.

- People who make icons will often make a bunch and post them with an invitation for everybody to help themselves. Don't just grab one and start using it, though – it's nice manners to first post a thank-you, say which one you took, and compliment them on their work!

- If you hang out on a particular group for a while, you're bound to end up making friends. Once you do, though, don't forget to keep the entire group in mind – always ask yourself if a post actually belongs in private mail or IM instead. Posts aimed at just a few people on the group are fine as long as they're kept in a clearly marked thread (e.g. *Chatboard meet up before the Leeds gig – the full report!!!*). But personal messages like *Hey tigergrrrl74, remember yr soup incident, lol* are boring and excluding for everyone else and really belong elsewhere.

- Be kind to newbies! If someone else violates any of the above, remember to give them the benefit of the doubt – they might not know any better. If you do decide to put someone right about something, be as gentle as you'd hope that someone would have been with you when you were a newbie!

Chat Rooms

Chat rooms have had a bad press for being dangerous, and indeed, they do call for extra caution (see p.54 for safety tips). Being so informal, there are very few rules to know, but it's worth remembering that:

- As with chat boards, the most helpful pointer is to listen in for a bit before you join in.
- Typing A/S/L? (Age/Sex/Location?) is common in many chatrooms as a way of breaking the ice and finding out exactly who you're talking to. But in some chatrooms, particularly those set up to discuss a specific hobby or interest, people don't do it, and it can be considered rude. In others, it's seen as an overtly flirty thing to say, rather than just a friendly thing, and may encourage people to give you a far more flirty response than you'd feel comfortable with.

Email

The joy of email is how informal it is, but it's still useful to remember these simple pointers:

- If you're writing an email to anyone other than a mate or relative, it's still worth bearing in mind the basic rules of letter writing. Make sure your emails are nice and easy to read by using spell-check and putting a space between paragraphs.

- If you're applying for a job or writing any other serious sort of mail to an adult you don't know, it's worth being a little more formal than you would in a regular email – for instance, use *Dear So-and-so* instead of *Hi!*

- You should always try to reply promptly to emails – you shouldn't really leave it longer than a few days at most. Having said that, it can be daunting when people send very long, chatty mails and you just don't have the time to write a long one back. The best thing to do is send a quick response saying how lovely it was to hear from them and explaining that you're just off to do something, but will mail back properly soon. Then make sure you do!

- When replying to a long email, try to resist the temptation to copy and paste the email into your new one and then intersperse it with your responses – it's the quick way of responding to a long mail, but it can seem quite rude and dismissive. Just imagine how you'd feel if you took the time to send a handwritten letter to someone and they sent it back to you with a few scribbled comments on it! Better to write a short but friendly reply instead.

- People often forget that an email address is as private a piece of information as a phone number or street address. You should always check with a friend before passing their email address on to someone else. For this reason, you should always be careful when sending out the same mail to more than one person. Most mail programmes have an option that allows you to hide the individual addresses, and you should use it! Equally, don't be tempted to mail someone if you've only got their address from a list on a group mail sent by a friend – first ask the friend to check with the other person if it's OK for you to have their address. And if you do email someone who didn't give you their address personally, you should always explain upfront in your mail who gave you the address, just as you would if you were phoning someone who didn't know you had their number.

- Be careful what you say in emails – you can carefully delete all your own emails, but that doesn't mean the people you send them to will, and you never know who might end up having a peek at someone else's computer. If you have something extremely private to say, say it on the phone or in person.

Group Mails

One thing that makes email so much more convenient than regular mail is the ability to share news, fun stuff and information with all your friends at the touch of a button. But be warned: Clumsy use of group mails can seriously affect your popularity! Don't forget that:

- Everyone hates wading through reams of junk mail, so always think before you hit forward. Something that may amuse one person will be just another piece of spam to someone else, so it's thoughtful to take a little more time and hand-pick who gets what, rather than sending everything to everyone.
- Some things should never be forwarded at all. As a rule, if

you didn't enjoy receiving something, you shouldn't pass it on. It sounds obvious, but it's amazing how many people pass on things that they themselves found scary, pointless, disturbing or threatening. Chain letters, for instance, should always be binned – at best, they're a waste of time and space, and at worst, you're essentially sending your friends a threat! If you're scared to break a chain, try a chain letters anonymous website – like http://www.csicop.org/chain – which allows you to send a chain letter to ten of their employees instead of saddling your own friends with it! Mails that warn of potential dangers and crimes in your home town can seem more important or helpful. Likewise, mails that ask you to forward them to as many people as possible for charity or to break a world record. But almost all of these are just urban myths, and are therefore a waste of time. Before you forward anything like this, it's always worth logging on to www.snopes.com and entering some key words from the story – you'll be amazed to discover almost every time that these stories are entirely made up and not worth clogging up your friends' mailboxes with.

- Forwards like funny pictures, jokes, quizzes and personality tests can be more welcome, but bear in mind that the person who sent you something may also have sent it to a lot of people you know. It's boring and annoying to receive things more than once so always carefully check the address list on the original mail before you consider sending it on to everyone in your address book.
- Be careful when hitting reply all on an email. If someone has sent out a party invite, their friends don't all need to know that you'd love to come!
- When sending attachments, always remember that not everybody has a mail server that can take big files. A hefty image or sound file could block or crash somebody's email client, use up the entire capacity of their inbox or take so long to down-

load that it delays them being able to get any other mail and has them cursing your name! For this reason, you should only attach a file if the person you're sending to is expecting it, and always avoid sending out group mails with attachments. If you're dying to show all your friends your holiday pics, or that cool little film clip you made, it's better to upload to a website (such as Myspace, Bebo, Photobucket, Youtube, etc.) instead, and send out a mail with a link.

• If you've emigrated, moved to a new area, changed school or just gone away on a long trip, it can be tempting to send regular round robins – newsy group emails. But it's worth being aware that people you're very close to might find round robins too impersonal and feel a little hurt, while those you're not so close to might find them boring and full of information they didn't particularly want to know! A better alternative is to send a small personal mail to the people you're closest to, then make a blog (on a site such as Myspace, Bebo or Livejournal) and send out a group mail with a link – then people can keep up with your news at their own pace.

MSN and Other Instant Messaging Systems

The casual, quick, throwaway nature of instant messaging means that manners are no big deal here, either. The only time things can get sticky is when you're holding a dozen conversations at a time – it's worth bearing in mind that one or more of the people you're talking to may be talking only to you, and feelings can end up being hurt if your slow responses make them feel ignored, especially if they're trying to tell you something important, rather than just having a silly, fun chat. Sometimes it can be better to explain to friends who have just come online that you're in the middle of an intense chat with someone else and can't talk right now, rather than trying to juggle lots of different conversations.

Home and Away

Having Guests to Stay

You love having friends to stay, and you always want them to enjoy it too, so that they'll want to come back again. Any pointers?

It's not hard to be a good host – it's as simple as making sure your guest is happy, and helping them to feel comfortable and at home. Helping someone feel at home doesn't necessarily mean letting them do everything their way (which isn't always possible or convenient). In fact, the easiest way to make someone feel comfortable is to help them to fit in with your routines. Bearing this in mind, it makes sense to bring them up to speed on everything they might need to know. You don't need to do it all in one go, but try to fill them in before they might need the information. Here are some things that it would be useful for your guest to know:

- What the usual time is for meals.
- Whether you dress for breakfast or eat in your night-clothes.
- What time you normally go to bed.
- Which household chores you're expected to help with (and whether you want any help doing them).
- Whether there is anything you have to do at a particular time – e.g. homework, watching your favourite TV programme.
- If any rooms are out of bounds to you (and therefore to them).
- If anything in the house is broken – a wobbly chair, a blocked loo, a door knob that always falls off. Otherwise

they might have an accident, and panic that the damage was their fault.

- Whether they're welcome to help themselves to snacks and drinks. (If there are some things which should be left alone, it's easier to ask your guest to tell you if they get hungry or thirsty.)
- Any information about the other people in your house – e.g. your granny is a bit deaf and has to be bellowed at; your dad is always foul tempered in the morning and likely to spontaneously combust if anyone speaks to him while he's reading the paper.
- About any noises that happen at night, which could be scary if you didn't know what they were: e.g. the neighbour's cat that knocks over the bins outside; the squirrels who scrabble around in your loft; your big brother who always climbs in the window when he comes home from the pub then wanders around the house singing football anthems and banging into things.

If your friend is staying for a few days or longer, should you give them a chance to have some time alone?

Only if they want it – and some people aren't that bothered. The simplest way to find out is to offer the chance of some time alone, and see if your guest takes you up on it – maybe you could say that you fancy going for a quick walk to the local shops, but that you don't mind if they don't want to come along. You should never assume that your guest wants time alone. In other words, don't ever tell them you're doing something without offering them the option to come along – that would be rude.

But what if you get invited out while your friend is staying and you can't bear to turn it down?

If you get invited out by another friend, you should tell them that you've got someone staying with you, and ask if it's OK to bring them along. If it's not OK (perhaps your friend had booked just two tickets for something), then you can't go – simple as that.

If you get invited on a date it's better to rearrange it right away for after your friend has gone home, because the person asking you out is unlikely to want your mate tagging along! You could ask your would-be date to bring along a mate for your friend – although if no one else thinks this is a good idea, forget it. No date at all is better than a double date where three out of four people are having a horrible time.

If you want to do something, and your friend doesn't, who should get their way? You (because it's your house) or your friend (because they're a guest)?

The only rule worth remembering is this: you shouldn't insist on doing anything that might make your guest feel uncomfortable. So if your guest doesn't want to do something because they might find it boring (like watch a programme you like on telly, which they don't like) it wouldn't be too devastating if you said you were going to do it anyway, and suggested that perhaps they could read or have a bath instead. But if you were talking about something like ringing up people you fancied and trying to persuade them to come round, it's a different story. If your guest wasn't into this, they could feel very uncomfortable, and to put them in that position would be thoughtless, so you should give it a miss.

If there's something you're allowed to do that your friend isn't, should you avoid doing it?

Tricky. Let's say you're allowed to watch the odd 18-certificate DVD now and again, but your mate's parents just don't allow it, and would go ballistic if your mate did. If you suggest watching an 18 film, you're putting your friend in a tough position, where they're at risk of getting into trouble with their parents, and maybe even jeopardising the chances of being allowed to stay with you again. But then, if your friend loves the idea and is desperate to see the film, it's their responsibility, not yours. You're their host, not their guardian. Safest to say, you should never talk someone into doing something they're not sure about, so if they're in two minds, you should step right in and say, 'Forget it, let's watch something else'. But if they're determined, and prepared to face the music (without laying the blame on you), then the decision is out of your hands.

What should you do if your friend breaks something or makes a mess?

Treat it as lightly as you can – accidents happen, right? Never do or say anything that might make your guest feel worse about the mishap – they probably feel horrendous already. Instead, do everything you can to make them feel better – tell them it doesn't matter (even if it does), help them clear up the damage, and tell your parents about it yourself (although you don't have to say it was your fault – that would be taking it too far!).

If they offer to pay for something to be repaired or replaced, should you take them up on it?

People usually only make these offers just to show how sorry they are that an accident happened, but hope that they won't be accepted, so you should turn them down. If you feel you want someone to pay, be aware things could turn a little frosty.

Visiting Other People's Homes

If you're allergic to animals, is it rude to ask someone to get their pet out of the room when you're in their house? Or should you just grin and bear it?

It's pretty impossible to grin when your eyes have mysteriously been replaced by big, damp, pink golf balls, so where's the sense in trying? You'd have a miserable time, your pet-owning pals would feel embarrassed and the whole situation would rapidly become a complete nightmare. Manners aren't about learning a set of rules and following them blindly. They're about using your good judgement to make every situation as comfortable as possible for everyone.

Is it OK to help yourself to a drink when you're thirsty?

If you're just visiting, you should always ask for a drink. Even if you're staying overnight or for a few days, it's still nicer to say, 'Would you mind if I got myself a drink?', even if you're just after tap water. Once your host has given you the OK, it's fine to help yourself to a glass and a drink. However, if drinking something means that there won't be any left for anyone else – if, say, there's a bottle or carton of something with hardly anything left in it, or just one can of something – you should always check with your host that they don't mind you having it.

What should you do if you're a bit peckish and fancy a snack?

If you haven't been invited round for a meal, it's a little bit cheeky to ask for a snack. But if you're starving and you know your hosts pretty well, you can probably get away with it, as long as you do it right. Here's how to be a hassle-free snacker:

- Don't raid the fridge without asking – not only is it rude but you might accidentally scoff an important ingredient for a planned meal.
- Don't just ask, 'May I have a snack, please?' or 'Is there anything I can eat?' – it puts your host to the trouble of thinking of something, and sounds like you're expecting them to make it for you.
- The most polite way to ask for a snack is to make it clear that: a) you're prepared to get it yourself, and b) you're not after any kind of huge gourmet nosh-up, just a mouthful or two of a household staple that won't be missed. Try 'Would you mind if I made myself a sandwich or have a couple of slices of bread and butter?' or 'Do you have an apple or a piece of cheese or something I could nibble on?'.
- Even if you're not expected to clear away or wash up at meals, you should always tidy up after yourself when you've made a snack, leaving the kitchen exactly as you found it.

What should you do if you accidentally make a mess in someone's house?

It's not bad manners to have an accident, just bad luck, so don't feel too terrible. The first thing to do is apologise. Be sure to sound suitably horrified – the bigger the mess, the more devastated you should sound. For instance, saying 'Oops. Oh dear. Sorry about that', sounds fine when you've made a muddy shoe-print on someone's hall floor, but not so good when you've just dropped a tray, six mugs of tea and a large cake onto their white sofa.

Don't flap around apologising for too long, though – the most important thing is to spring into action and set about tidying up. Ask where your host keeps the cleaning things, get some, and get to work. If your host would rather do it themselves, they'll say so.

If you make a mess while no one is around, do your best to clean it up. If there is any kind of evidence left – a stain, a still-broken item or whatever – you should tell your host what happened.

What should you do if you break or damage something?

It depends on the thing that got broken or damaged. Cups, plates and glasses tend to get smashed or chipped quite often, and most people will happily shrug this kind of thing off, as long as you apologise and pick up the bits. More serious accidents, like broken ornaments and scratched furniture, call for greater measures. First, make a really big apology. If no one saw the incident, don't be tempted to keep it quiet. Your host will notice, will assume that it was you, and will quite rightly be very cross.

When you're confessing, always explain how the accident

happened, but bear in mind that white lies are often better than the truth in these situations. Most owners of a broken ornament will get even more annoyed if the person who broke it shrugs goofily and says, 'Duh – I was just looking at it and I dropped it'. It's far better to look incredibly upset and say, 'I can't understand how it happened. I think I must have brushed past the shelf and it caught on my sleeve or something, and fallen off'.

Should you offer to pay for things to be mended or replaced?

Tricky. Most people would take your offer as nothing more than a very polite gesture, and turn it down. But you might be unlucky, and find that your offer is accepted, in which case you can't really take it back if you can't pay up! If you want to offer money, it's better to say, 'Can I give you something towards repairing or replacing it?' That way you'll be keeping your word even if you can only manage to fork out a tiny amount.

Eating Meals at Other People's Homes

Should you offer to help prepare the meal or set the table?

It's always nice to ask, 'Is there anything I can do?', because it shows that you're not just expecting to be waited upon.

If you're not sure what someone has just given you to eat, is it rude to ask?

It depends how you ask. Saying, 'What's this?' can sound pretty rude. Doubly so if you've got a look on your face like someone has just presented you with a bowl of sick. Instead, try commenting on how lovely the dish looks or smells, and then taking a wild guess about what it is: e.g. 'Mmmm, this looks great! Is it chicken?'. If you don't get as detailed an answer as you'd like, you could always ask your host how they made it. By the way, you should choose your guess carefully. Asking, 'Is this chicken?' won't offend anyone. Asking, 'Is this brains?' might.

I'm allergic to some foods. Will people get offended if I can't eat something they've made for me?

It makes sense to avoid the situation in the first place by warning people that you're allergic to something as soon as they invite you for a meal. If you forget, and you're pre-sented with a steaming plate of something that is your ticket to allergy city, you've obviously got to turn it down. Most people know how serious food allergies can be, and wouldn't have a problem – their logic would tell them that it's not your fault and therefore not worth getting cross about. However, there's something about several hours of slaving over a hot stove that can send logic out of the window. To be sure of keeping your host happy, it's also wise to make a big deal about how delicious the food looks and how devastated you are that you can't tuck in.

I'm vegetarian. What should I do if someone cooks meat for me? Do I have to eat it?

No, of course not. If you've made a choice to be meat free, other people should respect it. However, as with people who are allergic to certain foods (see above), it's up to you to make sure that you don't get into the situation in the first place.

Make sure that everyone knows you're vegetarian, and keep reminding them, particularly when they invite you round for a meal. It would be lovely if everyone remembered without needing to be reminded, but people have busy lives and bad memories, and although it's a pain, it's far better to tell someone for the billionth time that you're vegetarian than to be confronted with a huge roast dinner that they've spent hours cooking for you.

Is it OK to be a little bit picky about what you eat at people's homes if you're on a diet?

No, it's not OK. It's rude. If you're dieting, you should tell people as soon as they invite you round, saying something like, 'Oh I'd love to come, but I don't think I can because I'm on a diet'. If they really want you to come anyway, they can tell you, and you can feel free to eat cautiously, because you've already warned them. Otherwise, they can put off the meal, which they may want to do if they don't fancy making something low-calorie especially for you, or watching you pick feebly at their delicious food. Yes, you'll miss out, but at least you've avoided a sticky situation. But I think you should ask yourself whether your figure is really more important than your friends? Unless you're so overweight that your health is at risk, it's mad to let dieting rule your life.

So is it also rude to be picky if you're not hungry?

Well, it's always a bit off to leave food that someone has made for you, but you can't help it if you're not hungry – although you definitely shouldn't eat anything at home if you know you're going out to eat. The most polite way to get out of eating is to tell your host that you don't feel very hungry, so you'd just like a little serving of food. Eat a mouthful right away and comment on how delicious it is (even if it isn't), and try to force down another couple of morsels while everyone else is eating so that you're not just sitting there like a lemon. This only goes for main courses, by the way – it's OK to refuse dessert when you're not hungry.

Is there any polite way to avoid eating food that you don't like?

If you hate everything you've been served, it's quite hard to leave it without appearing rude, unless you're very good at acting and can convincingly pretend that you don't feel very well. If the thing you don't like is only a minor part of the dish, though, it's not rude to leave it and not mention it, as long as you eat plenty of everything else.

What if the food you hate is mixed in with everything else? Is it OK to try and pick it out?

It's not great manners, but it's better than not eating the dish at all. If you want to dissect your food like that, it's worth giving a fake reason. No one will mind if you casually say, 'This is delicious . . . I hope you don't mind me picking out these raw spring onions, but they don't agree with me/they give me indigestion/I'm slightly allergic to them'.

Is it OK to ask for seconds?

Sure. People who cook love to be asked if there's any more food going, because it proves how much you enjoyed it.

Should you help clear away the plates after dinner?

Some people don't like to clear the table until their guests have gone, especially at formal, organised meals, so if no one seems to be doing any clearing, you don't need to do it or even mention it. If your hosts are clearing away, though, it's nice to offer to help.

Using Other People's Loos

What should you do if you've used someone else's toilet and then found out that the flush doesn't work?

It can seem like the most mortifying thing in the world when you realise that the huge poo you've just done is going to stay in the bowl for all to see, can't it? Before you totally give up hope, though, it's worth waiting for the bowl to fill up with water again and trying another flush. Or if there's a toilet brush around, you can use it to prod the poo down the pipe and out of view, which sometimes works a treat. If there's a container of some kind around, you could also try filling that with water and pouring it into the loo, which sometimes works. Otherwise, just carefully drop a few sheets of loo roll into the toilet bowl to hide the contents and casually ask your host if they knew that the flush on their toilet wasn't working. Then forget all about it, because it's really not worth getting embarrassed about. Remember that: a) It's not your fault that the flush isn't working, and b) Everybody poos – it's no big deal.

What should you do if you've left a terrible smell?

Nobody's poo smells like roses – not even the Queen's, so it's no great crime. There's no need to mention it at all, as there's not much that anyone can do about it, and no one wants to discuss toilet-smells for fun.

The best way to avoid stinking up someone's bathroom is to close the toilet lid and flush as soon as you've finished. You could also open a window in the bathroom, if there is one (unless it's raining heavily – most people would rather have a stinky bathroom than a flooded one). If you do, you should make a point of returning to the loo to close it in half an hour or so, because if your hosts don't know that their window is open, they won't know to close it if it starts to rain later on, or for security overnight. Some people leave air fresheners or boxes of matches in their bathrooms (lighting a match makes the smell disappear like magic). If you find either of these things, use them. And if you're especially paranoid, you could even carry matches with you, just in case.

What should you do if you make a smell, or the flush doesn't work, and the next person waiting to use the loo is someone you fancy?

Tricky – on the one hand you don't want them to think you were the culprit, on the other hand, it's not exactly seductive to talk about toilet-things. I'd come bursting out of the toilet exclaiming, 'I think I'll wait and go later – whoever was in there last has blocked it!' as if I hadn't actually used the loo at all. But if they knew you'd been there a long time, then it's best not to mention it.

If you're staying at somebody's house and you have to use the loo in the night, should you flush the loo even if it might wake everyone up?

Most people agree that being woken by the sound of a flushing loo is worse than finding an unflushed wee in the morning, but not as bad as discovering an unflushed poo and a smelly bathroom. Therefore the unofficial rule is to leave night-time wees, but flush night-time poos. If you've got a guest bathroom to yourself, though, always leave the loo unflushed and let everybody sleep in peace. And whatever the situation, don't forget to go back and flush as soon as you wake up in the morning – with any luck, nobody need ever know you didn't flush in the first place!

If you find the toilet seat up at someone's house, should you leave it up?

Tradition has it that toilet seats should always stay down, so boys and men are expected to put them down when they've finished using the loo, and some girls and women get in a strop when they forget. It's kind of sexist if you think about it – why shouldn't men get in a strop when women leave the seat down? Still, that's the way of the world, and if you find the seat up, it's probably because the last bloke to use the loo forgot to put it down, so basically, even if you find it up, make sure it's down before you leave.

What about if you're a girl visiting a home where only men live? Should you leave the toilet seat up when you've finished?

I think so, yes – after all, this is the age of equality.

Staying the Night

I usually eat breakfast in my night-clothes and get dressed afterwards. Is it OK to do the same when I'm a guest?

Good house guests do whatever their hosts do – so if yours eat breakfast in their dressing-gowns, you're in business. If they don't, you should really get dressed as well. If you don't know what they do because you've never stayed before and there's no one around to check with when you wake up, you're better off getting dressed – you'll feel less silly being the only dressed person at a table of dressing-gown wearers than you would if they were all dressed and you weren't.

What should you do if you forget your toothbrush? Is it OK to borrow someone else's?

Uggg! No! Sharing toothbrushes is unhygienic, and even if you don't mind the idea, it's unlikely that anyone else will feel the same way. You could ask your hosts if they have a spare one – they might do – but your best bet is to just use tooth-paste and your finger until you get a chance to buy yourself a new one.

Is it OK to go to bed before your hosts if you're tired?

Absolutely. If you're tired, you're tired.

Are guests expected to do chores?

Different people expect different things but it's safe to say that most would expect you not to just sit around at dinner time while everyone else is clearing the table and washing up. Similarly, few would expect you to dash around wildly taking out the rubbish, cleaning the windows and scrubbing the toilet. If you offer help whenever it occurs to you, you'll soon get a good measure of how much is wanted.

What should you do if you stain the bed-linen?

Get the bed-clothes off the bed, bundle them up and ask your hosts if you can wash them. They're most likely to tell you not to bother, but it's still nice manners to offer.

What should you do if the friend you're staying with suggests doing something that you're not allowed to do at home?

If it's something you don't want to do, it's not at all rude to refuse to do it for this reason. However, if you do want to do it, and you're prepared to face the music if your parents ever find out, then the choice is yours. You should be sure, though, that your friend is actually allowed to do it – if they're not, you'll end up with both sets of parents being cross.

Longer Stays with Other People

Do you have to bring along a present when you're going to be staying with someone?

Yes, if you're staying for more than two days, bringing a present is really nice manners. It's a token thank-you gesture more than anything else, so it doesn't have to be anything big – most people bring something like a bunch of flowers, a little pot-plant or a box of chocolates. People generally give the present when they arrive, to start their stay on a friendly note. If you're really skint and your parents can't help out (and you don't have the time or facilities to knock up a little home-made something), it's not the end of the world. You can put the same message across perfectly well by saying a big, heartfelt thank you for the invitation, commenting on how kind it was of them to ask you, and telling your hosts how much you've been looking forward to coming.

Should you bring along something to keep you occupied while you're there, like a book or magazine to read or a hand-held computer game to play?

Yes, it's a good idea, as there will probably be times when your hosts won't feel like entertaining you, and they'll be more able to relax knowing that you're not at a loss for something to do. However, you should only whip out your book, mag or game if you're one hundred per cent sure that your hosts are planning on doing their own thing – it would be pretty unsociable to just plop yourself down in a corner and ignore everyone at any other time.

What should you do if you're not hungry at a meal time?

You should always sit down with everyone else while they eat and be a part of the meal, and it's good manners to ask for a small portion and at least have a couple of token nibbles.

If you find you're peckish later, you should really try to stick it out until the next meal. If you ask for a snack, you might not be hungry at the next meal either, and then it could seem like you're demanding to eat your meals when it suits you, rather than fitting in with everyone else.

Do you have to join in with everything your hosts do?

You should really join in with anything that involves leaving the home, because they probably won't want to leave you alone. If you refuse to go, they could end up deciding to stay in instead – and messing up other people's plans is horrible manners. However, if they're doing something that you can't do, are scared to do, or might get ill from doing (say, swimming, cycling, horse-riding, going on a boat), you don't have to join in as long as you explain exactly why, and you shouldn't feel bad about it. Still, you should offer to go along and watch, if that's possible. It's a different story, sadly, for outings that you don't want to go on because they sound deathly boring (e.g. food shopping, looking at an old cathedral). In these situations you just have to deal with it.

Activities that don't involve leaving the house are easier to duck out of, although it's still better manners to join in. If you really can't bring yourself to play tiddly-winks or watch several hours of riveting home-movies or whatever, you could probably get away with saying, 'No thanks', depending on what you do instead. No one will be offended if you sit quietly and read a book or magazine, write in a notebook, or doodle. If you ask nicely, they might not mind you going online on someone's computer to check your email or personal page (though do bear in mind that they might not have an unlimited-use deal on their internet connection, so keep it brief, as you would if you were using someone's landline.). Nor will they mind if you say you're tired and want to go to bed. It would be pretty rude, though, to do anything that might distract your hosts or spoil their fun – so playing video games, watching TV, talking on the phone, trying to start a conversation, poking at things in the room, pacing up and down looking agitated or sitting around sighing and sulking and looking as if you're about to keel over from boredom are all no-nos.

Incidentally, you should always give an opinion if you're offered a choice of things to do. Saying 'I don't mind' may seem like the polite option, but can actually make keeping you happy much harder work for your hosts, as they have to try and guess whether you actually do have a preference.

What happens if there's something you really want to do? Is it OK to suggest it?

Suggesting it is fine, as long as you make it clear that you don't want to be any trouble, and you won't be upset if the answer is no. In other words, it's not what you ask, but how you ask it. For instance, you will get a reputation for being a right royal pain in the backside if you say things like, 'I really want to go swimming tomorrow', 'I always lie in bed until at least eleven a.m. on Sundays' or 'I never miss an episode of *Doctor Who*'. Instead, kick off by asking a question to show that you're taking your hosts into account, for instance, 'Have you got things to do planned for every day this week?', 'Do you get up at the same time as usual on weekends?' or 'Do you ever watch *Doctor Who*?'. Once you've got an idea about where your hosts stand, you can tailor your next comment to suit. If they haven't got stuff planned/do lie in on weekends/do watch *Doctor Who*, you can chirpily reply, 'Oh that's great, because I'd really love to go swimming sometime/lie in on Sunday/watch tonight's episode, if that's OK . . .' If they've got a rigid agenda/always spring up at the crack of dawn/never watch *Doctor Who*, you're going to have to be more sheepish and make your suggestion sound more like a humble request.

If you can't do what you want, you should accept it as gracefully as possible (i.e. smile and say, 'Ah well, never mind . . .' even if you'd rather be lying on the floor screaming, or strangling them all).

A final word on the subject: when you're addicted to a TV show, it can feel like the world is caving in if you have to miss it. Since you shouldn't assume that you'll be able to do whatever you want at someone else's place, it's always wise to arrange in advance for someone to record it for you while you're away, just in case.

If you have other friends who live in the same area as the people you're staying with, is it OK to visit them?

It could be a hassle for your hosts if you march off anywhere on your own, because they're responsible for you, and will have to worry about how you'll get there and back, so it really depends on the situation. If you live in the same area too, or fairly nearby, and therefore could visit them anytime, then it's a bit rude to cause all that hassle. If you live in a different town, and don't get a chance to leave there often, it's more excusable. The other thing to take into account is who you're staying with. If you're with relatives or friends and there's no one of your own age-group around, it would be understandable that you'd want to visit a mate. But if you're staying with someone who is roughly the same age as you, you've basically been invited to keep them company, so you shouldn't really be nipping off and leaving them. If you really want to visit someone else, you should always take the friend or relative you're staying with, even if the two have never met before – it would be rude to leave them on their own.

If you go out shopping with the people you're staying with, is it OK to ask them to buy you things?

No – why should they? If you don't have any cash, those purchases will just have to wait – whether you're talking about a pair of shoes or an ice lolly. And don't kid yourself that heavy hint-dropping is any better than asking outright – it all amounts to the same thing.

Is there anything special you should do at the end of your stay?

Well, your hosts would probably be charmed and impressed if, on your last morning, you offered to strip the bed-linen off the bed you'd been sleeping in. Otherwise, all you should do is make sure you haven't left any mess for anyone to clear up, and don't forget to say, 'Thanks for having me' one last time.

It's also very nice manners to send a card, letter or email to say thank you, or make a special thank-you phonecall when you get home.

Socialising

Meeting and Greeting

What exactly are you supposed to do when you're introduced to someone?

Whoever you're being introduced to, you obviously want to make a good impression. If you're being casually introduced to someone of your own age, there's not much to it. You just:
- Look directly at the person you're being introduced to – not at the floor.
- Smile.
- Say something – anything. Even if it's just hi.

How about if you're introduced to someone older, or someone really important? Is it the same deal?

Yes, basically, but if you really want to impress, you can also:
- Stand up (if you were sitting down).
- Shake the person's hand. If they haven't put their hand out, it's fine to put yours out first.
- Say, 'I'm pleased to meet you' or 'How do you do?' (I know it sounds dumb, but don't worry – it's common. No one is going to say, 'How do I do what?').

Do you find hand-shaking a bit scary? Here are some tips:
- Always shake (or offer to shake) with your right hand – even if you're left-handed.
- If you realise when you're about to shake hands that your right hand is wet or sweaty, it's fine to subtly give it a quick wipe on your clothes before shaking. However, you should

never wipe your hand for any reason after you've shaken hands with someone – at least, not until they're out of sight – because it looks like you're trying to get rid of something that they transferred to your hand. Even if they did transfer something yucky to your hand, it would still be rude!

- When you're shaking hands, grasp the other person's hand firmly. If you let your hand and arm go all limp, it feels rather odd for them and makes you seem weak and wimpy.

How do you introduce yourself to someone?

You just stick out your hand in a shaking-hands kind of way and say, 'Hello, my name is . . .' If you're meeting someone much older than you, you should say your first name and your surname. If you're meeting someone of your own age and you want to be more casual, you can say just your first name, and you can also skip the hand-shaking bit.

You should always introduce yourself before you say anything else, whether it's 'What's your name?', 'Don't I know you from somewhere?' or whatever. And you should never ask someone 'Who are you?' – it's a bit abrupt!

What is the right way to introduce people to each other?

Here's the low-down, but don't get bogged down worrying about doing it wrong – the only thing that could actually offend people would be not introducing them at all!

- The basic form is to introduce both people to one another. In other words, you should say, 'Ella, I'd like you to meet Chloe. Chloe, this is Ella'. You could just say, 'Ella, meet Chloe' instead, and assume that Chloe is going to hear Ella's name clearly, but it might seem like you're giving Ella star treatment (she gets introduced to Chloe, but Chloe doesn't get introduced to her). It's not a big, big deal, but I think it's worth spending that extra couple of seconds to keep things equal.

- If you want to be really proper, you're supposed to use each person's full name – e.g. 'Ella, this is Chloe Brown. Chloe, meet Ella Smith'. If there are older people involved, this is worth doing, but otherwise, don't worry about it too much.

- There are a few rules about whose name you're meant to say first, but again, these are only worth thinking about in more formal situations. If you're interested, this is how you do it:
  - Women get introduced to men ('Ella, this is James Ross . . .')
  - Older people get introduced to younger ones ('Mum, this is Ella Smith . . .')
  - Important people get introduced to everyone else ('Dr Evans, this is Whoever . . .')

- If one of the people you're introducing is related to you, is your teacher or has some other specific relationship to you, it makes sense to slip the fact into the introduction, e.g. ' . . . this is my sister, Ella'. However, if you're introducing one friend to another, you should keep it simple and use just the names. For one thing, it would be a real mouthful to say 'My friend' before both names, but saying it before just one of the names implies that only that person is your friend and the other isn't!

- If someone is sort-of related to you, but it's all a bit complicated (e.g. your mum's live-in boyfriend's daughter, your grandpa's second wife who isn't actually your grandma), it's easier to just introduce them by name only, and explain your relationship in detail later, if you want to.

- When you're introducing people, be sure to use the name

that they like to be called by other people, regardless of what you call them. For instance, if your grandma doesn't like your friends calling her by her first name, you should say, 'Gran, I'd like you to meet Chloe. Chloe, this is my grandma, Mrs Jones.' The most common mistake that people make when they're introducing their parents is to forget to say a name at all, and just say, 'This is my mum'. This is obviously no good, because your mates can't call her Mum!

- If you're going to introduce two people and then leave them alone, it's nice to slip something into the introduction that will give them something to talk about once you're gone. You could point out an interest they have in common, or a person they both know (apart from you!) or just mention some interesting news about one of them (e.g. Chloe's just finished her GCSEs; Ella's just come back from holiday in Spain; James has just won a writing competition) – anything that they can pick up on so that they won't just be standing around in embarrassed silence!

When should you introduce people?

Any time that there are two people you know, who don't know one another, standing staring at each other! The only time you can safely give it a miss is if you're out walking with a friend, and you pass someone else you know – it's not rude to simply say hi and carry on along your way without stopping for introductions. However, if you stop to talk to the person you've bumped into – even for a quick 'Hi, how are you?', you should do the introduction thing, or else both your mate and the person you've bumped into will be standing there like lemons!

You should also always introduce people who are working for your family – decorators, cleaners, baby-sitters, etc. – to other people who come in. If you don't, it looks like you're sticking your nose up in the air and saying, 'Don't bother talking to the servants'. You should always introduce them by name, and never refer to them as 'our cleaner' or 'my nanny', which is rather rude and snobbish. If you want to explain who they are, it's much better to be straightforward, e.g. 'This is Liz – she looks after us until Mum gets back from work', or jokey, e.g.: 'This is Mary – she very kindly cleans up all the horrible mess we make!'.

How do you introduce someone to a group of people?

If it's a fairly small group – say, up to about six people – you should get everyone's attention then say something like: 'Everyone, I'd like you to meet Ella. Ella, this is . . .' and then say all the names, pointing as you go round. If there are more than six people, it would be pointless to go through everyone, because it would take too long and your friend probably wouldn't be able to remember all those names anyway! Instead, you should still tell everyone your friend's name, but only bother telling him or her the names of the people who are nearest. You can introduce the rest later, if you feel you need to.

What should you do if you need to introduce two people, but you've forgotten the name of one of them?

If you don't know them well, it's no big deal to say, 'I'm so sorry, but I've forgotten your name . . .'. If you really should know their name, though, and you're embarrassed that you've forgotten it, you could try and prompt them to introduce themselves by just introducing your friend to them, then

95

pausing. Or if you've got the guts, try, 'I'll let you introduce yourselves!' The only thing you shouldn't do is skip the introduction altogether – that's far worse than admitting that you've forgotten someone's name!

By the way, if someone ever seems to be struggling with an introduction, it's thoughtful to consider that they might have forgotten your name, and help them out of the spot by jumping in and introducing yourself right away.

What should you do if you've been introduced to someone, and you didn't quite catch their name?

It's no problem to ask them to repeat it. If they've got an unusual or foreign name, it's also not rude to ask them to spell it, or explain exactly how to pronounce it, as long as you use the right tone of voice. You want to sound as if you're saying, 'Wow what a great, unusual name!'

What is the best way to act if someone comes up to you and says hello, and you haven't got the faintest idea who they are?

Tread carefully. If they know you, then you must have met them (unless they've mistaken you for someone else, which doesn't happen that often). Bear in mind, then, that they might be pretty insulted to think that you've totally forgotten who they are. So if someone says to you, 'Do you remember me?', you should never say a straight no. Mind you, it's not a good idea to give a straight yes, either, because then they won't bother to say who they are, and you'll be struggling to think of something suitable to talk about while you desperately try and work out who on earth they are! Instead, try, 'I think so . . .' or 'Yes of course! But you'll have to remind me . . .' or 'I'm sorry, I'm terrible with names . . .'. If it turns out that you knew them years ago, then you're off the hook – you can just comment on how different they look now (hence you didn't recognise them right away). But if they turn out to be someone you really should have remembered, because it wasn't that long ago that you last saw them, it's thoughtful to try to invent some excuse for not remembering. 'I'm sorry – I'm not wearing my glasses/contact lenses' is always a winner (unless of course, you are wearing glasses!). Or you could ask some innocuous question like, 'Have you changed your hair?'. Considering that most people do something to their hair fairly often (and if they don't, it grows), the answer is probably yes!

If you're out with a friend and they run into someone they know, and they introduce you, should you wander off so that they can chat alone?

No, you don't have to – after all, your friend is out with you right now. If they want to talk to their other mate alone, they can arrange it for another time. If they start talking about something you're not interested in, though, it's not rude to wander off, read, or do anything else to occupy yourself until they're finished, if you want to.

V.I.P.s

It can be incredibly exciting to spot someone famous, and even better if you actually get a chance to talk to them. Just in case you find yourself in this nice position, here are some tips that should guarantee you a friendly reception and send the celebrity off feeling almost as pleased to have met you as you were to have met them:

- A lot of people tend to act as if they think celebrities are deaf, and stand very close, peering at them and saying things like 'I think it's her . . . Yeah, yeah, I'm sure it is!' This is intensely annoying, and will probably raise your chances of getting a frosty reception should you decide to eventually go up and talk with them.

- Try to work out whether a celebrity is on duty or off duty. If you spot them somewhere that they've been performing or filming or making a professional appearance, they are on duty and shouldn't mind you approaching them (unless they're grumpy or snobby anyway). If they're eating at a restaurant, shopping or wandering around, they're off duty, and don't really have any obligation to speak to you. This doesn't mean you can't approach them, it just means you should be extra nice and polite about it.

- Wait for a good moment to approach a celebrity, whether they're on duty or off – if you interrupt a conversation or anything else they're busy with, you won't get as friendly a reception as you might if you wait.

- Be thoughtful to the people the celebrity is with, whether it's their work colleagues, their friends or their family. Don't trample on them, shove them out of the way or totally ignore them. It's polite to nod a quick hello to them, and apologise for interrupting. Even if you don't particularly care what they think of you, you can bet that if you're nice to them, the celebrity will be nicer to you.

- If you want to ask someone for an autograph, always have a pen and a piece of paper with you. If you don't, it means that they'll have to scout around looking for one, or wait ages while you do, which is a waste of their time, and makes you look a bit goofy and thoughtless. If you have a pen and paper ready, it also makes it much harder for someone to refuse an autograph.

- When you're trying to figure out what to say, remember

that although you may feel like you know someone really well just because you've seen them on TV, played their music, watched their movies or whatever, you don't. A famous person is a stranger to you, and you shouldn't feel that you can say anything to them that you wouldn't say to any other stranger.

- Don't say anything at all negative, such as, 'All my mates give me a hard time for liking you because they don't think you're much good', 'You're not as good as you used to be' or 'You're fatter than I thought'. It's not only rude, but it will also make the person wonder why you bothered to talk to them in the first place.

- It's fine to ask questions as long as they're sensible, such as 'When is your next single out?', 'What was it like working with so and so?', etc. Don't ask rude personal questions ('How much did those sunglasses cost?', 'Is that your girl-friend?', 'Is that a wig?').

- Don't quote people's catchphrases or sing their songs to them – it's pointless and rather annoying.

- You should never take somebody's photo without asking their permission first. If someone says they don't fancy having their photo taken, you should accept it graciously and not take one – how would you like it if you weren't in the mood to have your picture taken (maybe because you felt that you weren't looking your best) and someone took one anyway?

- If you've nabbed some time with a celebrity, it's thought-ful to keep the meeting quick, so they can go back to doing whatever it was they were doing. This counts double if they were off duty.

Flirting

If flirting didn't exist, this planet would be an extremely dull place to live. Then again, people wouldn't get into half as many arguments and sticky situations, either. To guarantee virtually trouble-free flirting, you should stick to these guidelines:

- Don't flirt with your friends' boyfriends/girlfriends or dates.
- Don't flirt with their exes, either.
- Don't flirt with people who you know fancy you wildly, but you have no intention of ever dating.
- When you're on a date, don't flirt with anyone but your date.

Natural Bodily Functions

It's rather weird, if you think about it, that most natural bodily functions are considered rude to some degree, if you perform them in public. After all, everyone does them! Still, that's just the way it is, so here are some pointers:

Sneezing

This is the least rude of all the natural functions – it's quick, it's inoffensive, and even if it wasn't there's no way you can stop yourself from doing it! However, you've got to turn your head away from others and cover your nose and mouth when you do it, because if you don't, you end up spraying people with unpleasant goo from your nose and mouth – which isn't great manners.

Of course, if you've got a cold, sneezing can present bigger problems – namely, mucus. If you end up with a hand full of snot, your only option is to casually excuse yourself and dash to the nearest loo to sort it out with a bit of loo roll.

Coughing

You can't help coughing either, but again, turning your head and covering your mouth are essential. Also, if you're about to launch into a long, loud coughing fit, and you're in a situation where a big noise might disturb others (e.g. the theatre, the cinema, an exam room), it's thoughtful to nip outside as fast as you can and stay there until you're sure the coughing fit is over.

Blowing your nose

It's much better to blow your nose than let it run, so feel free to blow whenever you need to – as long as you've got a tissue handy. Turn your face away from other people when you're blowing your nose. The only time you shouldn't blow your nose is at the table, especially while other people are eating. And be sure to stuff used tissues in your pocket or up your sleeve – no one else wants to look at your dirty tissues, thanks.

Yawning

You should also cover your mouth when you yawn, although you don't need to turn your head. This is because although yawning doesn't send spray flying like sneezing and coughing, it does give everyone an eyeful of your tonsils, which no one is likely to be too enchanted with. Also, if you need to yawn while someone is talking to you, it's thoughtful to try and strangle it – they might assume that you're yawning because you're bored, which would be insulting!

Burping

Unless you're at home, or with close mates only, you should always try to stifle a burp. If one escapes by accident, cover your mouth and say 'Pardon me' or 'Excuse me' afterwards.

Farting

Needless to say, farting in public isn't generally acceptable, but then, you probably wouldn't want to do it anyway! If you accidentally let one rip, just pretend that it didn't happen. If someone else smells or hears it, keep cool. If you just shrug and say you can't smell anything or didn't hear anything, the conversation will be dull enough that no one will want to continue it. If you start making a big deal ('Pwoooar! Yeah, who did that? Pooo-eeee! That's disgusting!') the conversation will go on for longer, and you'll just feel more embarrassed. The same goes for wildly denying that it was you or frantically accusing other people of being the perpetrator. If there is no way you can pretend that you know nothing about the fart (say you did a really, really loud one), just say 'Oops, sorry', as if you'd just burped. There's not much anyone else can say after that, and it'll be far less humiliating.

If someone else farts when you're around, it's also thoughtful to minimise their embarrassment in the same way. In other words, ignore it, rather than wondering out loud what that terrible smell is, making jokey comments, or – worst of all – directly accusing them of farting.

Going to the loo

This is one natural function you should never perform in polite company. Always use a toilet.

Home Truths

If someone has their flies undone, food stuck in their teeth or loo roll stuck to their foot or something, should you ignore it in case you embarrass them? Or is it better to tell them?

It's definitely more thoughtful to tell them, because if you don't, they'll find out for themselves sooner or later, and be embarrassed anyway. In fact, they could even be more embarrassed, because it'll dawn on them that they had food in their teeth/loo roll on their foot/their underpants proudly on display the whole time that they were talking to you!

You should break this kind of news very casually and gently. In the case of undone flies, you can get away with making an ahem noise and pointing in the general direction of their nether regions – universal body-language for 'Your underpants are on show, mate'. In other cases, you'll probably have to speak. Try, 'Ooh, I think you've got something stuck in your teeth/on your foot . . .'. The idea is to minimise the embarrassment, so make out like you only just noticed the thing. And always say 'something' rather than loo roll or spinach or half a packet of hula-hoops – when you start getting specific about the offending item, it sounds much sillier, and also gives the impression that you've been staring at it for ages (which you have, but you don't want to let on, do you?).

Should you also always tell people personal home truths too, like if they have bad breath or B.O.?

Not always. As a rule you shouldn't break this kind of news to anyone you don't know very well, or to anyone much older than you, even if you do know them well (like a teacher, for instance). Basically, you just have to keep quiet, hold your nose, and hope they figure it out for themselves soon. However, it's thoughtful to tell a close friend this sort of thing, if you feel that you can. If they don't sort it out, the day is bound to come when some idiot says something insulting or teasing about it to them – which is obviously a far worse way to find out about it. Imagine yourself in their position – if you had a problem which could be sorted out, wouldn't you much rather know about it so that you could fix it, than carry on through life with people talking about it behind your back?

So what's the best way to break this kind of news?

Very, very gently and carefully. (So if you thought it would be a top idea to say, 'Hands up everyone who doesn't have bad breath . . . Er, put your hand down' forget it.) White lies and tricks are the order of the day. Here's a good one: pretend that you haven't noticed the problem at all and drop useful hints instead. For instance, you could blow into your cupped hands, sniff loudly, then make a yuck-face and say, 'Bleeugh! Don't you find that if you forget to brush your teeth and use mouthwash every morning your breath really smells?!' If this fails, you could try and pretend that the problem is not a long-term one. For instance, you could exclaim, 'Ooooh, did you eat something spicy last night? Your breath smells a bit funny!' before suggesting this wonderful brand of breath-freshener you always use every morning, just in case.

If a trick doesn't work first time, wait a while, then try again. With any luck, the penny will drop. If not, gather your courage and have a gentle but straightforward heart-to-heart.

What should you do if someone asks your honest opinion about something personal, but hearing the truth might upset them?

Good friends do tell the truth. They just dilute it sometimes. For situations which aren't earth-shatteringly important, the best thing to do is guide your friends in the right direction without telling things exactly as they are. A little nifty word-play is all it takes. For instance, if you're shopping with a friend and they ask you, 'How do these jeans look?', they won't thank you for saying, 'About twenty sizes too small and completely ridiculous'. But if you say, 'Nowhere near as nice as the ones you've got already, and they're way too expensive . . .' you're warning them off the dodgy jeans without being mean.

For more serious situations, though, forget the pussyfooting around and tell nothing but the truth. Let's say a friend is dating a two-timing, mean-spirited pig, and asks for your opinion. It would be crazy to lie, or spout some meaningless fob-off when you could be boosting your friend's confidence and saving them a lot of heartache by telling them that they deserve better and you wish they'd stop letting people walk all over them. Get the idea?

Favours

Few things put more of a strain on relationships than borrowing or lending things. Being good at borrowing is a useful skill. People who aren't good at borrowing soon find that no one wants to lend them anything. A good borrower:
- Never borrows stuff without asking first.
- Always gives things back as soon as they've finished with them, well before the lender has a chance to ask for them back.

- Always gives things back in exactly the same condition as they were when they were borrowed – or even in better condition.
- Never makes the lender come over to get their possession back.

If someone lends you an item of clothing that needs washing or ironing, does that mean it's OK to give it back unwashed? I mean, it's in about the same condition as when you got it, isn't it?

No. If you've worn something, you should always clean it, regardless of how it was when you got it.

What are you supposed to do if you accidentally damage something you've borrowed?

Basically, you've got to fix it, and tell the person who lent it to you what happened – even if the damage is totally undetectable.

What if the damage is so bad that it can't be sorted out at all?

The bad news is that you really should dig into your pocket and buy a replacement or, if you're broke, offer to give the lender something similar of yours.

Even if the thing you borrowed was old and on its last legs to start with?

No, if the thing you borrowed was already on its way out, it wouldn't really be fair – and if the person who lent it to you is a reasonable sort, they'd probably agree, and be prepared to forget all about it. Unfortunately, not everybody is reasonable, and you could end up having a wrangle on your hands, which is why it's best to avoid getting into these situations in the first place. If you're about to borrow something a bit old and dodgy, think twice.

How about if the damage wasn't your fault? What if something just breaks while you're using it?

Unfortunately, when you've borrowed something, it's your responsibility, so it's still up to you to put things right. You could argue with the lender, but they're unlikely to believe that their possession just spontaneously broke without you doing something to it, so you'd have to be prepared for a bit of an argument.

If someone has lent you stuff in the past, are you obliged to lend them things they ask for?

Obviously if someone has lent you something, they've done you a favour, and that means you owe them one. However, it doesn't mean that they can name any favour they like and you have to fulfil it, like it or not. If they ask to borrow something you really don't want to lend – because you want to use or wear it yourself, or simply because you can't bear to part with it, even for a few days – there's no reason why you should have to give it up. Still, you should say no as nicely as possible. In other words, explain that you know you owe them a favour, explain why you don't want to lend them the thing they want to borrow and suggest some other thing they could borrow from you, or some other favour you could do them.

Eating

Golden Rules of Table Manners

We all know about table manners. So why, then, from time to time, do we all find ourselves in situations where we're not sure what to do? In a minute, we'll check out the most common puzzles, but first, just in case you've had a memory lapse, here are the golden rules of table manners:

Use your knife and fork properly

Don't cut up all your food into little chunks, then eat it bit by bit – cut off pieces as you go. Don't take a big forkful of something, then bite off half of it – take smaller forkfuls instead, and put the whole lot in your mouth at once.

Don't do anything which looks piggy

Encircling your plate with your arm as if you were guarding it with your life is not on. Neither is stuffing in huge mouthfuls, taking a mouthful of food before you've finished chewing the last lot, taking a sip of drink while there's still food in your mouth, wolfing your food down very fast (ideally, try to finish at roughly the same time as everyone else at the table), frantically cutting up food while you're chewing, lifting up your plate or bowl so it's closer to your face or lowering your head to the plate when you eat (you should sit normally, head up and bring the food to your mouth, otherwise it looks like you're used to eating out of a trough). When you've finished eating, don't lean back and say something like, 'Phew, I'm stuffed!' or 'Wow, do I feel sick now!'.

Don't do anything annoying

Avoid making ear-battering noises (e.g. scraping your chair across the floor, scraping your knife or fork on the plate). Don't fiddle with or pick at anything on the table – that includes playing with melted wax from candles, messing with vases of flowers, prodding at or rearranging decorative centre-pieces, making swirly patterns in spilled piles of salt and pepper or doing anything with sauce bottles or salt and pepper pots (e.g. juggling or using them to represent you, your best mates and that really fit exchange student when explaining exactly what happened at the school disco last week).

Don't do anything gross

Anything that could put people off their food is O–U–T. That includes making a big mess, picking your nose, ears, teeth or nails, blowing your nose (go to the loo and do it), making snotty hawking noises, talking with your mouth full, chewing with your mouth open, making noisy munching sounds and noisily slurping soup or drink. Also think carefully before bringing up yucky topics of conversation for the same reason – that great story about how you found a cockroach in your salad on holiday, or the time your baby brother's nappy exploded in the supermarket should be savoured after dinner.

Don't do things you're supposed to do in the bathroom

It's fine for girls to re-touch their lipstick when they've fin-ished eating, but doing a complete make-up overhaul isn't.

Nor are grooming activities like combing your hair and cleaning under your nails.

Don't be unsociable

It goes without saying that you're not supposed to do any-thing that makes you ignore everyone – like read, write, doodle, talk or text on your mobile (even reading texts is out), listen to an MP3 player or play a hand-held video game!

How do I know where to sit when I'm eating out? Do I just sit anywhere?

If you're at someone's home, stand near the table until some-one tells you where to sit. If no one says anything, ask whoever seems to be in charge of the meal where they'd like you to sit. If they say they don't mind, you can take your pick. The same goes for meals at restaurants if you're being taken out by an older relative, a friend's parents or anyone else who has organised the meal themselves.

What exactly are you supposed to do with napkins?

If you're eating anywhere fairly smart, you might find a cloth napkin in front of you. Here's everything you ever wanted to know about napkin protocol (sounds thrilling, huh?):

- Well before any food turns up, unfold the napkin and lay it across your lap. Don't tuck it into your collar or anything like that.
- The napkin stays on your lap until you've finished eating all the food (including dessert), but you can lift it up to wipe your mouth during the meal, if you want.
- If you go to the loo during the meal, you lay the napkin

next to your plate and put it back on your lap when you come back.

- Don't use your napkin for wiping dirty plates, glasses or cutlery at a restaurant – if something is dirty, ask for a new one.
- Don't blow your nose on it either.
- When you've finished the meal, you just lay the napkin on the table beside your plate, or if your plate has been taken away, in the centre of the table.
- If you get given a paper napkin, you should stick to the above rules as well, but it's not as important.

Should you start eating as soon as you get served your food, or wait for everyone else?

The popular rule is that you can start right away if the food is hot, but if the food is cold, you should wait until everyone's been served. Having said that, it's generally more polite to wait, either way. It means that you can't go wrong – if the people you're eating with always wait for one another, you haven't botched-up, and if they're not bothered, they'll tell you to go ahead and start.

What do I do if I drop my knife or fork on the floor?

Pick it up, lay it on the table and ask whoever is serving up the food for a new one. If it happens at someone's home, and you know them very well, and know where the cutlery lives, it's fine to offer to go and get it yourself.

Never carry on eating with cutlery that has hit the deck: even if you're relaxed about germs, other people might not feel the same way, and watching you gaily chow down using something that's been on the floor could put others off their food.

Why aren't you supposed to put your elbows on the table?

Actually, it's not the big deal it once was. By and large, you shouldn't rest your elbows on the table while you're actually eating because it can look a bit lazy and slouchy, but no one is going to mind if you do it before, after and between courses.

I know you're not supposed to lean across people at the table, but what if you really need to?

I can't honestly think of a situation where you would really need to. If you want something that's out of reach, ask the person nearest to it if they could pass it to you. If someone asks you to pass something to them because you're nearest to it, but handing it to them would mean leaning over someone else, you can ask the person next to you if they could pass it on.

By the way, if someone asks you to pass them something edible (such as a bread roll), always offer them the whole bowl or basket so they can take one out themselves – you should never handle anything that someone else is going to eat. And no, saying ''scuse fingers!' while you do it doesn't make it OK!

Is it OK to dip bread into soup or use it mop up leftover sauce?

Soup, no – unless you're at home, or at someone else's home where everyone else is doing it. Sauce, yes – as long as you do it delicately and try to avoid wiping the plate completely clean (which looks a bit piggy).

Is it OK to spit out something I don't want to eat?

Bottom line: you want to avoid spitting anything out. So if you get a mouthful of something too hot, or something you just don't happen to like the taste of, it's best to be brave and swallow. However, if we're talking about something you honestly can't swallow because it's inedible or just plain disgusting – a bit of gristly meat, a bone, an unidentified object or something that definitely tastes off – then getting it out of your mouth is perfectly OK, as long as you do it right. Ejecting food across the table with a loud 'Pah!' isn't great manners. Nor is spitting it directly onto your plate whilst making vomiting noises. Instead, raise your hand to your mouth, quietly spit the offending thing into your hand, then discreetly plop the contents of your hand onto the side of your plate. If you've got a paper serviette you can spit into that instead, then screw it up and tuck it next to your plate. Either way, don't make a big fuss, and don't prod or study the stuff you spat out, unless you're convinced that it might have been a bug, a piece of glass or something else that shouldn't have been in your food.

So what should I do if I find something horrible in my food?

Ideally, you should avoid making a great big deal about it while other people are still eating. If you're eating out, wait until everyone's finished, then tell your waiter – you deserve an apology at the very least, and you may even get some money off the bill! If you're at someone's house, however, it's a different deal. If you think you can manage to ignore it, do. But if it was horrible enough to kill your appetite, your host will probably wonder why you suddenly stopped eating, so you should tell them. Bear in mind that if the food was home-made, the person who cooked it is going to feel really terrible, so you should be ultra kind. Tell them it's not a problem, that it was an accident which could happen to anyone, and that you're really not too bothered about it (even if you feel like you're on the verge of chucking up all over the table).

Help! How Do I Eat This?

Everyone has times when they run into edible things that they're not sure exactly how to tackle – it's nothing to be embarrassed about. The best rule is to watch someone who looks like they know what they're doing and copy them. It's also worth boning up on how to deal with some of the most common things which get people puzzled. Here they are:

Bite-sized things which aren't really bite-sized

When you haven't got a knife and fork to eat with, but something looks too big to fit in your mouth in one go, it's no problem to eat it in two bites.

Sandwiches and burgers at places with cutlery

At home or at a fast-food place you'd obviously eat them with your hands, but these days a lot of restaurants serve them, and it can be puzzling to work out whether to use your knife and fork or not. Generally, you should use the cutlery, as dumb as it may seem, especially if other people at the table are eating meals that do need to be eaten with a knife and fork. If you just feel too ridiculous, you could probably get away with eating your burger or sandwich with your fingers, as long as you use your cutlery to eat whatever was served alongside it (including chips). Whenever you're eating with your fingers anywhere but at home, remember not to lick anything off them – use your napkin instead!

Olives

The right way to eat olives that have pips in them is to stick one in your mouth, eat the edible bit, then discreetly bring your hand to your mouth to spit out the pip. If there isn't a little bowl or plate that's been put out especially for the pips, pop yours on your bread plate (at a restaurant), into an ashtray or – if there's nowhere else – onto the table. Never put the pip back in the bowl of olives.

Bread rolls at restaurants

Break the bread with your hands – you don't need to cut it. Then butter one piece at a time before you eat it. If there's a knife on or near your little side plate, that's the butter knife. If there is only one fork beside your plate, but two knives, then the one furthest from your plate is the butter knife. Ditto if there are two forks and three knives. If you've only got one knife by your plate then it's fine to use it for buttering.

Un-shelled prawns

Not for the squeamish! To get to the prawn itself, you first need to get a good grip on the little leggy bits on its under-side, and pull them off. Once they're off, the rest of the shell comes off easily, leaving just the head (aaargh!). Grasp this in one hand, and the body in the other, give a tug and bingo! – your prawn is totally undressed and ready to be eaten. All this should be done with your hands, by the way – it's just too tricky with cutlery. Put the discarded bits on your plate, or in the spare bowl provided, if there is one.

Whole fish, or fillets on the bone

If you get served a whole fish, try to avoid shrieking, 'Eeeeuuuw! It's got eyes!'. Once you've overcome that hurdle, cut off the head and tail, push them to the side of your plate, then get the top fillet off the bone that runs through the middle. The easiest way to do this is to slice long-ways down the middle, then slide each half off the bone. Once you've eaten these bits, you can either flip what's left over and do the same thing again, or carefully lift the bone off and shove it to the side of your plate before eating the bottom bit.

Finger bowls

If you're served food that you eat with your fingers, you some-times get given a little bowl of water with a piece of lemon floating in it. This is for dipping your fingers in to wash them before wiping them on your napkin. Don't drink it!

Chopsticks

If you've never learned how to eat with chopsticks, don't panic. Firstly, it's not that hard, and someone you're eating with will be glad to show you how to do it. Secondly, no one is going to turn their nose up if you ask for a knife and fork instead.

When you're eating with chopsticks, the key is to take only little bits of food at a time, so there's less chance of dropping it. Never use a chopstick to spear food, and unless you're with close friends only, and try to avoid the temptation to stick your chopsticks under your top lip and say, 'Look! I'm a walrus!' for a laugh.

Eating at Restaurants

How do you get a waiter's attention?

Try to catch their eye or give them a friendly little wave. If they're rushed off their feet you might have to call out, in which case you can call, 'Excuse me!' loudly enough to be heard. 'Hello!' is OK too, but yelling, 'Waiter!' (or 'Waitress!') is a bit rude, as is barking, 'Oi!', 'Hey!', 'You!' or 'Over here!' Snapping your fingers in your server's direction is also a complete no-no.

If you want something during the meal, you should always try to find the waiter or waitress who has been serving you. Although it's tempting to grab the nearest server rather than wait until yours is free, you shouldn't, because although they will help you, they're busy looking after their own tables, and they're not being paid to help you – the money from the service charge or tip will go to your server.

Who should order the food?

Usually, everyone orders their own. It used to be the done thing for a girl out with her parents or a date to tell her dad or date what she wanted to eat, so that he could order for both of them. You can still do that if you like, although these days most waiters ask each person individually what they would like, starting with the females at the table. If that's the case, it would obviously be rude for a girl to ignore the waiter's question!

How do I know which knives and forks to use if there are more than one set?

You work from the outside in – in other words you use the

knife and fork furthest from your plate to eat your starter. When you're finished, you put them together in the centre of your plate and they get taken away. When your main course turns up, you use the set that's left. If there are more than two sets (as there sometimes are at weddings and very posh dinners), it just means that you'll probably get more than two courses. If there is one more knife than there are forks, the extra one is your butter knife. You can leave it on your side plate when you're done with it.

If everyone has ordered different things at a restaurant, is it OK to offer people a taste of your food, or ask to taste theirs?

Yes, as long as you know the people you're eating with fairly well, and as long as you do it politely. If the person whose food you want to taste (or vice versa) is sitting next to you, the best way to swap tastes of food is to use your own fork to take a bit of food off their plate, and clear your knife and fork out of the way so that they can help themselves to a bit of yours. If they're opposite you, and you know them well, it's fine to get a bit of food on your fork and hand it over to them. Incidentally, if you know the person very well, it's not rude to actually feed them a piece of food, but bear in mind that it's a rather flirty thing to do with someone of the opposite sex – so if you don't want to send out flirty signals, don't do it! If there are lots of people at the table, and you're miles away from the person with whom you want to swap food, it's probably better to scrap the whole idea – it's not great manners to be passing forkfuls of food or big plates up and down the table!

What do I do if I get given a fork and spoon to eat dessert with?

The general idea is to hold the fork in your left hand (if you're right-handed) and use it to keep the dessert from flying off the plate while you cut off and eat bits with your spoon. However, it's all right if you want to use just one or the other.

Are there any special rules to follow if I'm being taken out for dinner by someone else as a treat?

First, it's thoughtful to check out the prices on the menu before ordering, so that you can avoid ordering a dish that's wildly expensive (although if all the dishes are roughly the same price, give or take a couple of quid, don't worry about it. Similarly, it's OK to order an expensive thing if the person who is paying is having the same thing, or something which costs the same amount). Secondly, if you don't like the food much, keep it to yourself, if you can – it's a bit rude to whinge about your meal when you're being treated. Finally, don't forget to say thanks – it's nice to do it twice: once when you've started eating ('Mmm – this is lovely – thanks so much for bringing me here'), and again at the end of the meal.

If someone invites me to go to a restaurant, does that mean they're going to pay for the meal?

It depends. If an older relative, or the parents of a friend invite you to eat out with them, then they would almost certainly be planning to pick up the bill. If someone asks you on a date and takes you out to eat, they probably should pay, but it's nice manners to offer to pay for half (and be prepared to cough up if your date takes you up on your offer!). If you've agreed to go out with a group of friends, then you should expect to split the bill equally, regardless of who suggested the meal, and regardless of who invited who.

If my friends all ordered much more than me, surely I shouldn't have to pay the same share as them?

Unless you had just one course and everyone else had two, then yes, you should. There's nothing more annoying and confusing than someone adding up what they've had and stingily insisting on paying only for that. Another exception would be that if one person ordered much, much more than everyone else, or ordered a very expensive dish – then they should put in a little bit more. Otherwise it's best to keep it simple, as nothing spoils an otherwise fun meal than spending hours juggling numbers and fiddling around with cash. Of course, if all of you agree that you'd like to pay for only what you ate, and you can stand the hassle, then go ahead.

But what happens if I don't have enough money to pay for more than what I've eaten?

You wouldn't have much choice, really, would you? You'd just have to explain and hope your friends don't mind.

What happens if I don't have any money at all?

Unless you're certain that someone else is going to pay for a meal, you should always take some money out with you. If you're strapped for cash, you should think twice before going at all. Otherwise, be sure to tell the person who invited you about your situation right away. If you say, 'I'd love to come, but I haven't got any money at the moment', they can either let you know that they'll pay for you (in which case you can relax and enjoy the meal without worrying about what's going to happen when the bill comes), or make different arrangements. Whatever happens, you should never let yourself get into a situation where the bill turns up and you have to explain that you can't pay.

But what if I just forget to take any money out with me, by accident?

In that case, someone else is obviously going to have to pay for you. You should always ask nicely if they'd mind doing it and thank them wildly – even though they haven't got much choice! Once someone has paid for you, you should always pay them back as soon as possible, the next day at the latest. Never say, 'I'll get the next one!' – they weren't expecting to lend you money (which is essentially what they've done), and they might not be able to afford to be out of pocket until you go out to eat together again.

Cafés and Fast-food Joints

Are there any rules about sharing tables?

In cafés, cafeterias and fast-food places where there are no empty tables about, you've got every right to share someone else's – especially if you've already bought your food. But just because something is your right, it doesn't mean you should be aggressive about it. Choose the table with the most room, and ask whoever is there already if they mind you joining them – don't just plonk yourself down without asking. And remember that although people should always let you share their table, they don't have to, so you should return their kindness by showing them a bit of respect. In other words, it's not fair to do anything that could annoy them – e.g. spreading your stuff out over the whole table, shrieking, singing, snogging, talking very loudly, telling rude jokes, discussing things that could be offensive, smoking or making a big mess with your food or drink (unless it's an accident). If you've let someone else share your table, you can expect whoever joined you to follow the same rules. If they don't, feel free to ask them to stop doing whatever it is that's annoying you.

If you're eating in a café, cafeteria or fast-food place, is it OK for one person to queue while the other grabs a table?

If the place is pretty much empty, it's fine. Otherwise, the answer is a big NO. People who are already in front of you in the food queues should have first call on the tables, since: a) they were there first, and b) they might end up standing around with heavy trays of food, desperately looking for a table, their food getting cold, when you haven't even got yours yet – very unfair, right?

For hints on eating at buffets and posh sit-down do's, see *Parties* (p.139). You'll also find everything you ever wanted to know about eating at other people's homes in *Home and Away* (p.76). And finally, if you want to know more about tipping, flip to *Out and About* (p.165).

Parties

Invitations

Getting invited to a party could mean anything from receiving a letter containing a gold-embossed card written in full toff-speak, to someone tapping you on the shoulder and saying, 'Oi! You! My place! Saturday night! How about it?' But no matter which end of the posh-scale (or anywhere in between) the invitation falls, the rule is the same: you've got to let the person who invited you know whether you're coming or not. Ideally, you should do your responding in a way that is appropriate to the kind of invite you got.

- Most written invitations say RSVP – which, as you probably know, stands for *répondez s'il vous plaît*, French for please reply. However, if there is no RSVP, you should still reply. The chances are that it's only missing by accident.

- If there is a residential address or email address written under the RSVP, it means you should reply in writing. If there is a phone number too, you could reply by phone instead – but if the invitation looks kind of posh and formal, you're better off writing. (The number might only be there for last-minute cancellations.) Unless you're emailing, you should always write a handwritten reply to an invitation, rather than a word processed one.

- If there is only a phone number under the RSVP it means that you're expected to phone rather than write – although obviously no one will be offended if you write instead!

- When you're writing a reply to an invitation, make sure it's in a similar style to the invitation. For instance, if an

125

invitation says: *Mr and Mrs Henry Poshington-Bottomly request the pleasure of your company to celebrate the 16th birthday of their daughter, Caroline . . .*, it wouldn't be a hot idea to whip out your cute notepaper and scribble *Dear Caz, yeah I can come. Cheers.* You should always write directly to whoever is inviting you (in this case, Mr and Mrs Poshington-Bottomly), and mirror the style. You'd write your address on the right (or middle), their address on the left and if you can go, you'd write: *(your name) accepts with pleasure your kind invitation* or *(your name) is delighted to accept your kind invitation.* If you can't go, you'd write: *(your name) regrets that (s)he is unable to accept your kind invitation.* If you feel weird doing this, because Caroline is a really close friend, you can send her a friendly note or phone her up as well, but you should always reply properly to a formal invitation.

- Verbal invitations, whether they're over the phone or in person, are generally much simpler. If you know on the spot whether you can come or not, you're sorted. If you're not sure, you should let the person who invited you know one way or another as soon as possible. Do it in person, if you have a chance, or, if you're unlikely to be seeing them for a day or so, do it by phone, text, instant message, email, carrier-pigeon — basically, whatever is going to be the fastest way to get hold of them.

- Verbal invitations can get confusing when someone invites you to a bash, you tell them you can come, and then an invitation mysteriously turns up in the post. Are you meant to reply again, or what? For informal parties, you sometimes get a written invitation just so that you've got a record of the time, address and other details you'll need — in other words, you don't have to reply. If, however, the invitation looks pretty formal, the verbal invite was probably just to check out whether it was worth sending you a proper invitation — so you should reply. If you're in any doubt at all, reply, just to be safe.

• If you've agreed to do something official at a function, like being a bridesmaid or pageboy at a wedding, or making a speech at a friend's barmitzvah (Jewish coming-of-age celebration), you might still get an invitation. However, you don't need to reply to it – in these cases, they're usually only sent to you as a souvenir of the occasion.

Help! What Shall I Wear?

Deciding what clothes to wear to a party is pretty stressful. Pick the wrong thing, and you can end up feeling so uncomfortable that you don't enjoy the party!

So how do you know what sort of clothes to wear to a party?

Before you make a decision, it's always a good idea to talk it over with someone else who is going. Better still, talk to the person who invited you. The most important thing is to take into account what kind of party it's going to be.

Let's say it's a friend's party, round their house?

If the party is being thrown by someone around the same age as you, at their house, you don't need to worry too much about being under-dressed, and the most important thing is to choose something you're going to feel comfortable in. If you don't feel comfortable in party clothes, you should go casual. Not lying-around-watching-cartoons-on-a-Saturday-morning-eating-cereal-out-of-the-packet casual, but the kind of clothes you'd wear out on an after-school date – attractive and nice, but low-key. Of course, if you like dressing up, and you feel happy in your dress-to-impress clothes, then go ahead and wear them, as long as you're sure you won't feel funny if some of the other guests aren't equally dolled-up. It's worth remembering though that feeling over-dressed is much worse than feeling under-dressed.

What if the party is a big, organised event?

In that case, you'll probably have received an invitation, and some invitations have a dress code written on them (see opposite). Otherwise, you have to look for clues. Is the invitation itself very swanky? Where is it being held? Is it evening or daytime? The swankier the party sounds, the more effort you should make to dress up. If you're frightened of over-dressing, play safe by choosing something that's smart, clean and new-looking, but not too over-the-top, and do your hair nicely. This way you can avoid the very horrible embarrassment of being over-dressed, but you'll at least look like you've been respectful enough to make an effort, so no one can rightfully be funny with you about it. Remember too that people are prepared to give teenagers a bit of leeway – you can usually get away with wearing things that adults can't.

How about a wedding?

If there is no dress code on the invitation, look at where the service and reception are being held, and at what time. For instance, you can usually get away with smart but informal clothes for weddings where the service is at a registry office, the reception is in someone's home or the celebrations look set to finish before dinner. But for a religious service, a reception in a hotel or a dinnertime do, you should go for something a bit dressier. Either way, never wear jeans or trainers, scruffy stuff, sports clothes or casual shorts. As a general rule, wear formal or semi-formal clothes (see below). Tradition also has it that no one should wear all black (it's supposed to be bad luck for the couple getting married), and girls shouldn't wear all white or cream (because it looks like they're competing with the bride).

Dress Codes

Dress codes are guidelines for what to wear, although some of them are so vague that they're not that much help! Here's what they all mean:

White tie

This is the most formal of all dress codes and means that males are supposed to wear an especially snooty get-up which includes a tail-coat, white waistcoat and white bow-tie (most people hire the whole caboodle from a dress-hire shop). Girls and women are expected to wear extremely glamorous dresses – long ones, ideally.

Black tie

This is very up-market too, and means that males must wear dinner suits (a particular style of black suit), with a dress shirt, a bow-tie and either a waistcoat or a cummerbund (a kind of wide, fabric belt). This get-up is also sometimes known as a tuxedo, which is its American name. Again, most people hire these clothes. Females should go for cocktail dresses – either short or long fancy frocks made of an eveningy-looking fabric.

Formal

This means some kind of smart suit, shirt and regular tie for guys, although younger boys can usually get away with a tailored jacket and trousers instead of a suit. Girls can wear any kind of smart dress. For a formal daytime event, they can go with a suit instead, or a smart top (like a shirt or blouse) worn with a smart skirt or tailored trousers. Incidentally, tailored basically means a piece of clothing that is smart-looking because it is structured, a classic formal shape and length, and made from some kind of fairly posh-looking fabric – so, basically, not jeans, cords, cargo pants, trackie bottoms, denim skirts, hoodies, anything with a logo or slogan printed on it, or anything unstructured, frayed, clingy or stretchy.

Semi-formal

This is when things start getting complicated. Boys can go for suits or tailored jackets and nice trousers (not jeans, tracksuit bottoms or baggy pants). Girls can go for just about anything that isn't a fancy frock, but is smarter than day-to-day wear.

Smart-casual

This means any casual clothes that look clean and presentable, except tracksuits, shell-suits and other sporty items. Jeans are OK if they're new-looking (not faded or ripped), and if you wear them with a nice shirt or sweater. T-shirts are OK if they're clean and ironed, and if you're wearing a smart jacket over the top. Shorts are OK in the summer if they look tailored – in other words, not made of denim or lycra. Girls should avoid teeny-weeny shorts, skirts or dresses that show a lot of leg, especially if the event includes a religious ceremony (e.g. a wedding or christening). If you're desperate to wear something tiny, at least wear opaque tights with it. Both sexes should wear proper shoes – not trainers – although you could probably get away with boots if they were very clean and new-looking.

Informal or casual

These are tricky categories, because what they mean depends on who wrote them. Some people's idea of informal or casual clothes is exactly the same as smart casual (see opposite), and they'd be horrified if you turned up in clothes that you think of as casual. Other people would be perfectly happy to see you in the clothes you'd wear to knock around with your friends. You just have to use your own good judgement, but your safest bet would be to lean on the smarter side, just in case.

How to Be the Perfect Party Guest

The secret of how to be a good party guest is very useful knowledge. Why? Because the better a guest you are, the more parties you'll get invited to. Sounds good, eh? So read on . . .

Good party guests always:

- Arrive on time and leave well before the host wishes they would.
- Offer to help tidy up if they're still around towards the end of a party.
- Stick around the main area where the party action is going on.

- Keep personal noise at the same level as the general noise going on around them and keep dead quiet outside when they're leaving.
- Do their best to fit in with everyone else and behave in a way that's acceptable for the situation.
- Do everything they can to make the party go well – like introducing people who don't know each other, and encouraging everyone to dance and have fun.

. . . and never, ever:

- Arrive early or are one of the last to leave.
- Start tidying up in the middle of a party unless they've broken or spilled something.
- Sneak around other areas of people's homes, especially not to nip off for a kiss and cuddle in a bedroom.
- Do anything that would get the party-giver in trouble with their neighbours – like turn up the music, shout or scream (even if someone drops an ice-cube down their back).
- Launch into pulling, telling dirty jokes, smoking or drinking booze if no one else is.
- Spoil the party mood by sulking, crying, being nasty, having an argument, or taking the mick out of people who are dancing and having fun.

Is it OK to bring a date to a party?

There's no set rule, so unless you're a mind reader, you'll need to ask the person who invited you. Don't get heated if they say no, though – it's likely to be for a good reason. Maybe they're trying to keep the numbers low, maybe they don't like the idea of having people they don't know well at their party, or maybe they invited you because they had other unattached people coming to the party that they wanted you to meet. If you can't get hold of the person who invited you, don't bring the date. In fact, you should never bring anyone (be it a date, a friend, your Belgian penpal who is over staying with you, whoever) along to a party without checking first. It's wildly rude, and you might end up not getting invited again.

Should you wait to be offered a drink at a party, or can you help yourself?

Most people leave drinks out so that people can help themselves. If you can't see anything out, or it all seems to have run out, it's fine to ask your host for a drink. You shouldn't ever help yourself to drinks from someone's fridge – it may not be the drink for the party, but for the host's family, and it would be pretty rude to use it.

What happens if there's no food at a party and you're starving? Can you ask the host for a snack?

I'm afraid not. If someone hasn't organised food for a party, it's because they didn't want to go to the trouble and expense. If you ask for a snack, you're putting the host in a spot – on the one hand it's no trouble to slip you a couple of slices of bread and butter or something to keep you happy, but on the other hand, if everyone sees you eating, they might want some too, and then what?

If you've been invited to two parties in one night, is it OK to go to both?

The most polite thing would be to go to just one – going to both is not so much a matter of keeping both hosts happy (they'd both rather you stayed with them the whole time), but of having your cake and eating it too. If you really want to go to both, you should let the hosts know beforehand that you plan to leave early or arrive late. A good tactic is to call and explain that you suddenly remembered that you'd already agreed to go to another party the same night. Obviously this will be a white lie in the case of the one you were invited to first, but it sounds better than saying, 'I've been invited to another party and I want to go to that as well'. By the way, if either of the parties were big, formal affairs, you really can't go to both – you're supposed to arrive at that kind of function on time and stay until it's all over.

Is it OK to change the music at a party?

If someone is acting as DJ, then no – whether they're a proper DJ, or just a friend of the host, it's up to them what is played. If everybody seems to be taking turns putting stuff on, then you could probably chip in, but it's polite to try and stick to music that's similar to what's being played already. In other words, don't put on a slow-dance track when everyone is enjoying getting sweaty to faster stuff, and vice versa. And a party is never a good time to play your favourite weird, obscure new musical discovery – try to stick to stuff that the majority of people will know and like.

Is it OK to kiss at parties if other people aren't?

If no one seems to be doing it, it could make others pretty uncomfortable if you start having a game of tongue-hockey with your date, so it's best to hold off and judge the general mood a bit later. If the lights go down and the music gets smoochy, snog away.

If people are drinking alcohol at a party, is it rude not to join in?

No way! Not at all. Anything to do with your body is your personal choice, and nothing to do with manners. Just as it's not rude to refuse to let someone be intimate with you if you don't feel like it, it's not rude to refuse to do something that could potentially damage your body – like drinking, smoking or taking drugs – if you don't want to. Anyone who thinks you're being stuck-up or a spoilsport by giving these things a miss is a prat, and their opinion doesn't count for anything. It's also not rude to leave the party altogether if people give you hassle for abstaining, as long as you tell the person who invited you why you're off.

What should you do if you accidentally break or spill something?

If you're at someone's home, deal with it right away. If it's a spill that won't leave a stain, just grab a cloth from the kitchen, wipe it up, put the cloth back and forget about it. If it's a spill that probably will stain, damage to furniture, or a breakage, tell the host right away, apologise like mad, then set about clearing it up as best you can. Offer to pay for major damages if you want, but don't get into a big long angst-ridden ramble about it in the middle of the party – suggest to the host that you sort it out after the party or tomorrow. Of course, if they want to sort it out immediately, do. (For more, see *Home and Away* – p.75.)

If you're at a party venue, as opposed to someone's house – for instance a church hall, a youth club, a hotel reception room – you needn't worry so much. Everyone expects the odd spill on the floor, chairs or tables, and the occasional glass or plate to get broken, and it's no big deal. Just tell someone who works at the venue what's happened and offer to help clear it up (although your offer will probably be turned down). If the situation is more serious, you should tell the host what has happened as well, because any charge for the damage will probably get stuck onto their bill.

If someone asks you to dance, and you don't want to, how do you turn them down without being rude?

Hmmm. Tough. Very tough. You see, it's not rude to turn down a date with someone you don't fancy, because a date takes up quite a hefty chunk of your spare time, and time is too precious to waste on things you don't want to do. But a dance? Come on, it's only a minute or two out of your life, so turning down a dance is a bit like saying, 'I don't even like you enough to spend a couple of minutes with you, thank you'. In other words, however nicely you decline, you're still sticking your middle finger up and blowing a raspberry – so if you want to be a nice person, you should be brave and dance. If you'd really rather die, just saying a friendly, 'No thanks' does the job best. Don't get into making excuses ('I can't dance!', 'I'm tired!', 'I've mysteriously lost all sensation in both my legs!', etc.) unless you're not going to dance with anyone at all, all night. Telling lies is a really vile thing to do.

None of the above applies, however, to invitations to dance to smoochy music. Slow-dancing is a far more intimate proposal: it usually involves having someone's body right up against yours, their arms round you, and your faces very, very close together. No one should ever have to do anything intimate that they don't feel one hundred per cent comfortable with, so if you don't fancy getting that close to the person asking you, it's perfectly polite to turn them down.

Fancy Dress Parties

If you get invited to a fancy dress party, do you have to go in fancy dress?

Yes, because the person throwing the party certainly will be, and you can be sure that most others will make the effort too. If you turn up dressed normally, the host could feel insulted that you didn't bother. Besides, if everyone is dressed up at a fancy dress party, no one feels silly. But if someone turns up in regular clothes, the dressed-up party-goers could feel self-conscious – and it would be rude to spoil other people's fun by making them feel stupid.

If you throw a fancy dress party and someone turns up in normal clothes, would it be rude to send them home?

Yes! If you've invited someone to a party, you should never turn them away! Don't tell them off either. Perhaps they forgot the party was fancy dress, or maybe they're painfully shy. Even if they just couldn't be bothered, or are too vain to make themselves look silly, telling them off will ruin the atmosphere of the party. Instead, smile warmly and insist that they let you help them get kitted out in something more unusual now that they've arrived. This is worth doing, because your dressed-up guests might feel uncomfortable if someone is roaming around looking normal, and the normally-dressed guest is likely to feel uncomfortable too – and if people feel uncomfortable, the party won't go as well as it could. If the party is at your home, it's a good idea to sort out some emergency costumes beforehand.

If you don't have any suitable clothes, you could rustle up some sheets to be worn as Roman togas, or take a tip from one great party hostess I know, whose fancy-dress rule is that anyone turning up dressed normally has to wear one of her swimsuits (whether they're male or female). If the party isn't at your home, you should still be able to find a little token item for your normally-dressed guest – perhaps one of the other party-goers has a spare mask or other little something from their costume? Failing that, wrap them in toilet paper and tell everyone they've come as an Egyptian mummy.

Wedding Receptions

Can you bring a date to a wedding?

No – only the people whose names are written on the invitation can go. You can't even ask if it's OK to bring a guest, either – you can be sure that it's not OK, and you shouldn't put the bride or groom in an embarrassing spot by making them tell you themselves. Remember that weddings are very expensive and difficult to plan, and if every guest wanted to bring someone extra, the budget, the table plans and everything else would swiftly be up the creek, as it were.

I've noticed that when you arrive at wedding receptions, the bride, groom and their family are often lined up at the door. What are you supposed to say to them?

Just something cheerful and deeply boring about how nice the service was, how lovely the bride looks or the weather ('Nice day for it!', 'Shame about the rain!'). Or you can just say congratulations. Whatever you say, make it brief. Even if one of the people in the line-up is a friend, save long chats till later on, or you'll cause a traffic jam!

Sit-down Do's

A sit-down do is any big, celebratory party-thing where all the guests sit down for a meal, grouped round largish tables. Wedding receptions, anniversary parties and barmitzvahs are often organised like this. In case you're not sure what to do with yourself at one of these do's, here's the general idea:

- When you arrive, check out the seating plan – a big board with everybody's name and table number on it. Remember which table you're supposed to be at, so that you can go straight there when you're told to sit down.
- When you find your table, your place will be marked by a little card with your name on it.
- Introduce yourself to anyone at the table who you don't know.
- There will often be starters and bottles of soft drink on the table when you get there. It's fine to help yourself to a drink (don't forget to offer it round to other people at the table before pouring your own), but don't start chowing down on the food until you're told to.
- Once the meal is over, there are often speeches and toasts (more on those later). Once they're over, you're free to get up and do whatever you like.

If you don't like or know the people you've been put with, can you ask to be moved, or just switch your place card with someone?

No, sorry. It took some poor person hours to work out the seating arrangements, so there's no way you can even think about messing it up. Basically, you just have to deal with it until the meal and speeches are finished.

Can you start eating as soon as everyone at your table has been served, or do you have to wait for everyone in the whole place?

There is usually a head table at these things, where the bride and groom, the anniversary couple, the barmitzvah boy or whoever else's party it might be, sits with their family. The tradition is to wait until everyone at this table digs in. However, they are often served first, and may have started eating by the time you get served anyway, in which case you should just wait for the other people at your table.

Can you go and talk to people at other tables between courses?

You shouldn't really, because you'd get in the way of the people who are frantically trying to clear plates and serve food.

There always seems to be a lot of standing up, sitting down and making toasts at these things. How do you know what to do?

You stand up when someone says something like, 'Please be upstanding' and sit down again when everyone else does. When someone proposes a toast, you're supposed to wait until they've stopped blathering on, then raise your glass, repeat the name of whoever is being toasted (e.g. 'The brides-maids!', 'Rose and Albert!'), then take a sip of your drink. You don't have to clink your glass against other people's.

Buffets

A buffet meal is far less frightening than a sit-down affair, but it can still be a bit baffling at times. Here are some pointers:

- The first thing to do is check out whether there are any plates about. If there are, get one. If not, it means all the food is designed to be picked up and popped directly into your mouth.

- At a no plates buffet, the food is there as a snack to nibble on in between chatting or dancing or whatever, rather than as a proper meal. Bearing this in mind, you shouldn't hoard loads of food in your hand or pockets, then scuttle off and stuff your face. Nor should you stand by the buffet table for ages and ages cramming things in your mouth and generally hogging the food. Yes, it's tricky if you're ravenous.

- Once you've got a plate, you've got to work out whether you're supposed to serve yourself or not. Needless to say, if there are people hovering around behind the buffet table holding serving implements, then it's their job to do some or all of the dishing up, and you're expected to tell them which food you fancy. If not, work your way along the table, helping yourself.

- Walk away from the buffet table before you start eating. If there are tables and chairs available to eat at you should sit down to eat your goodies; otherwise, it's fine to dig in standing up.

- If you're holding a drink and a plate, and there's nowhere to sit, eating can be rather tricky. If you don't think you can balance your glass and plate in the same hand without decorating your chest with punch and coronation chicken, don't even try. Instead, find a flat surface to set your drink or plate on while you nibble, or stand near a wall and put your glass on the floor by your feet (where it won't get kicked over) until you've finished eating.

- Don't pick up a piece of food while you're still chewing another – it has a distinct air of desperate, piggy face-stuffing.

- Never put something back on a serving plate once you've picked it up.

- If you're eating dip, only use the crisps, vegetables or whatever else has been put out especially for dipping – not your fingers, fork, or any other piece of food from the table. Dip each item only once, no matter how big it is – sure, it's a drag to be left with a big, boring bit of carrot once you've bitten off the yummy dipped part, but sneaking it in for a second visit to the dip is just not on since it's been in your mouth, and no one is going to particularly fancy dunking their food in dip that's been mixed with your spit.

Hosting a Party

All you need for a great party is a little bit of space, a lot of great music, a bunch of friendly people who want to have a good time, plenty of refreshments, and a host who knows what to do. And here's what every host should know:

A good host always:

- Plans ahead carefully, making sure they've thought of everything, even for a last minute, spur-of-the-moment party.

- Makes sure that their guests are having a good time, and does their best to keep everyone in a party mood.

- Introduces people who haven't met and tries to give them something to talk about, like pointing out a hobby or interest they have in common.

- Spots any bad feeling between guests and steps right in to sort out any trouble long before it starts.
- Makes sure that there are plenty of refreshments available and that everyone knows where they are.
- Keeps the music going at all times.
- Gets their closest friends to help them with all the hosting duties.

. . . and never, ever:

- Realises too late that something essential is missing.
- Gets so wrapped up in having a good time themselves that they don't have a clue if everyone else is or not.
- Fails to notice if a guest is standing around alone with no one to talk to.
- Lets guests argue or snipe at one another in front of everyone else, ruining the party mood.
- Needs it pointed out to them that the supply of refreshments is running low and needs refilling.
- Plays the same CD twice or leaves long silences between tracks.
- Gets so frantic running around that they forget to enjoy the party!

Special Occasions

New Babies

When someone has a baby, do you buy a present for the baby or the parents?

People generally send or give a congratulations card to the parents, and buy a little thing for the baby – a cuddly toy, something to wear, whatever. This is probably because it's far more fun to shop for baby things! If the new baby has older brothers or sisters, it's also thoughtful to buy a tiny token present for them too, so they don't feel that the new baby is getting all the attention. Of course, if they're family friends or relations, your parents will probably deal with all this on behalf of the whole family.

Is it rude to ask someone whether their baby is a boy or a girl? Are you supposed to be able to tell?

Some parents do get pretty touchy if you ask, and even touchier if you guess and get it wrong, which is pretty crazy, because it *is* hard to tell. If you can't guess from the clothes (some people still go for pink and frills for girls, blue for boys), there are two good tricks.

Knowing the baby's name usually sorts the problem out (unless it happens to be a weird, made-up or unisex name!). To avoid saying his, her or its (which can get parents even more wound up than getting the sex wrong), either ask, 'What's the baby's name?' or play cute and ask the baby, 'What's your name?' directly.

Failing that, you can follow a rather sexist rule that many nurses are taught: refer to the baby as she, and if the parents correct you, smile and say, 'Oh sorry, he's just so pretty, I thought . . .' That way, even if you're wrong, you're being flattering.

Weddings

Do you have to give presents at a wedding?

Oh yes, definitely. Here are some pointers:

- If you've been sent a joint invitation, asking you to come with your parents, or with a boyfriend or girlfriend, you only need to buy one present between you. If it's with your parents, they'll probably buy one from all your family.
- If you've been invited to a wedding, but you can't go, you can still send a present, although you don't have to.
- The present should always be for both the bride and the groom, even if you only know one of them.
- You shouldn't spend more than you can afford on a wedding gift, but you should still try to choose something which is just that bit more extravagant than a birthday present.
- Some people have a wedding list at a particular shop or department store. This means you can visit the store – or sometimes even go online – to find out which things the couple would like to get as a present (usually household things like kitchen gadgets, crockery, towels . . . yawn . . . you get the picture). The choice will range from the cheap to the expensive. Once you've chosen and paid for your present, the store will wrap it, write a label to say it's from you, and deliver it to the bride and groom with all their other gifts.
- If there's no wedding list, you have to choose something yourself. Most people go for bits and bobs for the home

that don't need to match anything else (like vases, ornaments, unusual kitchen things, etc).

- People usually send their wedding present to the couple before the wedding. If the couple live together, you send it to their home. If not, you send it to the bride's home or the bride's parents' home. You can also send the present after the wedding, although if it's way after the wedding, you should scribble a note explaining what took you so long!

- Another option is to take the wedding present with you to the wedding reception (but not to the service!), where you ask one of the wedding attendants (the people who show everyone in) where you can leave it. You never hand the gift directly to the bride or groom or ask them to come and open it – they're much too busy!

(For the low-down on what to do at wedding receptions, see *Parties* – p.138)

Religious Ceremonies

How are you supposed to know what to do if you get invited to a big religious event and you don't know anything about the religion?

Don't panic – no one will expect you to know exactly what to do. No matter what the event, you can't go wrong if you dress smartly, are polite, smile a lot, and copy someone who looks like they know what they're doing. If you're really nervous, you can always ask the person who invited you if there's anything they reckon you should know beforehand.

Deaths

What are you supposed to do when someone you know has someone close to them die?

If the bereaved person is someone you see a lot, you should definitely talk to them about the death, but you can write to them too. If you're not likely to run into the bereaved person soon, it's usual to write a special letter to them, called a letter of condolence. Whether you write or talk, here are some handy hints:

- A letter of condolence written to an adult should really be an actual letter – handwritten, and sent by post. Writing it on a card, rather than a piece of plain writing paper is fine (though you should only use special condolence cards, which are easily found in any shop that sells greetings cards), but email is best avoided as most adults are likely to find it a bit casual under the circumstances. If the bereaved person is your age, and a close friend, you could send an email instead, but bear in mind that they might be too upset to be checking their mail, especially if the person who died was someone they were very close to. At least if you send something by post, you know they'll definitely get to read it in the next couple of days.

- You usually start a letter of condolence by saying *I'm so sorry to hear about your sad loss*. If you're speaking to the person, it's usual to start by saying, 'I'm so sorry . . .'. I know this sounds like it was your fault that the person died, and you're apologising, but it's a well-known phrase and it's fine.

- Most people go on to write or say things like *I'm thinking of you*, and *Please let me know if there's anything I can do*.

- After that, write or say whatever you feel. If you can't imagine what it's like to lose someone you love, say that. If you don't know what to say, you can say that too.

Deaths

- If you're close to the person you're writing or talking to, it's nice to mention something personal, like a happy memory you have of the person who died. You can do this even if you never met them: e.g. 'I know I never met your granny, but I always smile when I think of that funny story you told me about her dancing on the table at your cousin's wedding. She sounded so cool.'
- Always stick to the subject – it's not the time to write or talk about yourself and your news, however important.
- Don't make jokes or try to be funny – these letters and chats are for expressing sympathy, not for cheering people up.
- Never make wild statements that the bereaved person may not agree with (e.g. 'He was so ill, I'm sure he's quite glad to be dead', or 'I'll bet she's in heaven, playing with your cat').
- You should write letters of condolence as soon as you hear about the death, before the funeral if possible.
- If you're face to face, it's thoughtful to ask a bereaved person if they feel like talking about their loss. Most people find that far from making them sadder, talking helps them to cope better. If they don't want to talk, at least you'll know – but tread carefully when you change the subject. It would be thoughtless to say, 'Oh, OK then. Did you see *EastEnders* last night?' Instead, let the bereaved person change the direction of the conversation or end it altogether.

Once when a friend told me that her granny had died, I started laughing, and I don't know why. She was really upset and I didn't know what to say. What should I have done?

You know, it's very, very common to feel an urge to laugh when someone tells you something bad. It doesn't mean that you find it funny, it's just a strange, nervous reaction that sometimes happens when you feel shocked or very emotional, and you just can't help it. When this happens, it's important to explain right away that you don't actually find the bad news funny – in fact, you feel very sad and shocked – and that you don't know why you're laughing. If you apologise, and say that the last thing you want to do is cause more upset, there's no need to feel bad.

Are you supposed to give presents at a funeral?

No, but if you want, you can send traditional funeral flowers – like white lilies – or a wreath. You send these to the undertakers who are arranging the funeral. Another tradition is to make a donation to the dead person's favourite charity – some families ask well-wishers to do this instead of spending their money on flowers. Yet another tradition is to make some food – something sensible that can be heated up like a pie or lasagne – and take it round to a bereaved person's house, so that they don't have to bother with cooking while they're in a state and busy arranging the funeral. If this all sounds a bit practical and grim, and you'd rather give something that would cheer the bereaved person up, that's fine – but you should wait until after the funeral.

What should you wear to a funeral?

The look you're going for is sombre and respectful. Wearing black or another dark colour is traditional, but the style of your clothes is the most important thing, and should be as smart as possible. Bright colours, crazy patterns, T-shirts with funny slogans on them and any clothes that are scruffy, trendy or sexy are not on.

What are you supposed to say to the dead person's family?

Basically, the 'I'm so sorry . . .' bit (see p.148), and if you knew the dead person well, you can also say something about how much you'll miss them, and how lovely they were. Funerals can be very emotional events, though, and it's often hard to say anything. If you're stuck for words, everyone will understand. And remember that sometimes, giving a hug or a putting your arm gently around someone's shoulder can say everything you want to say just as well as any amount of words.

Christmas

What's the deal with Christmas cards? Do you have to give them to all the people who give you one?

Yes, that's the general rule. Whether you follow it or not is up to you. On the one hand, there's no point in spending time and money on sending a card to someone you don't actually give a stuff about. On the other hand, Christmas is traditionally a time for being kind and thoughtful, even when it means doing things that are a pain in the backside. If the person who sent the card would be overjoyed if you sent one back, and heartbroken if you didn't (e.g. a lonely old relative, the smelly unpopular kid at school who gave the whole class a card), you should get scribbling.

Is it offensive to send a Christmas card to someone who is of a different religion?

It shouldn't be. These days, sending a Christmas card is simply a friendly greeting, and not really a religious thing at all. However, you should try to play down the religious angle, by avoiding cards featuring nativity scenes, churches, etc., or ones which have a religious message inside. Pictures of Santa, holly, Christmas trees or presents and Merry Christmas messages are unlikely to upset anyone, but if you want to be really safe, go for something with a snowman or a snowy street scene on it, and a really neutral message, like *Happy Holidays* or *Season's Greetings*.

What should you do if someone gives you a Christmas present and you haven't got them one?

If you really wish you had got them a present, or you've genuinely forgotten to get one, tell a white lie (e.g. you left it at home, you could have sworn it was in this bag). Then get something and give it to them later. Otherwise, just say a big thank you, and add, 'I'm so sorry I haven't got anything to give you'. That's fine.

If you're visiting a boyfriend or girlfriend's house on Christmas Day, do you have to give their family presents?

You don't have to give individual presents, but you should definitely take something. Food, flowers or a plant would do fine.

Birthdays

Why do some adults act so funny when you ask them how old they are on their birthdays?

Up to a certain age, getting older is exciting. Some people carry on finding it exciting all their lives, but quite a lot of others find the thought of getting older depressing. For people who feel like that, birthdays are extra depressing, because they're a reminder of this. In other words, then, it's their problem – so don't take it personally. But it's thoughtful to make a mental note not to ask them again next year!

Presents

What should you do if you can't afford to buy someone a present?

There are very few people who would be petty enough to get annoyed if you gave them a card and explained that you were too short of cash to buy them anything. People are particularly understanding at Christmas, when the sheer number of presents to buy puts a serious strain on everyone's finances. It is a good idea to tell them well in advance so they don't get you a present. For birthdays, the important thing is to show that you remembered the occasion – so a card is a must. If you really can't afford even a card, find a scrap of paper and draw one. If you can't draw, decorate the paper with pictures cut out of a magazine. Anything will do, even if it looks rubbish, because it shows that you cared enough to make the effort. In fact, a handmade card can be even nicer than a shop-bought one, because it's so personal.

If you want to give a gift, there are ways to rustle one up for free, with a little time and imagination. For instance, you could:

- Cook something. Most people can manage to find a recipe and the basic ingredients needed to bake up a cake.
- Write a token that can be cashed in for a favour. On a nice clean piece of paper, write or type, *This token entitles (name) to . . .* and then write in something suitable that you don't mind doing. Adults would appreciate having their car washed or their little kids baby-sat. Brothers and sisters would love an offer to take over all their household chores for a week. A friend might like the chance to borrow something of yours for a bit, such as a nice item of clothing that they've admired, a video game, a DVD, your bike, whatever. Use your imagination.
- Give away something of yours. In many eastern countries it's a tradition to give a friend an item of clothing or jewellery that belongs to you. The thinking behind it is that: a) you're showing how much you care because you're giving up something you like, and b) the hippy-dippy spiritual part – when you give away something you've worn, you're giving your friend some of your positive energy. If you tell your friend about this tradition, and give them something nice of yours, they're bound to be really touched – especially if it's something that you obviously like because they've seen you wearing it. By the way, socks and underwear are out!

Is it OK to buy the same present for more than one person?

It's fine at Christmas, because everyone understands that you don't have time to go traipsing round a billion different shops, or choosing loads of different gifts. Birthday presents, however, should be more personal, and have more thought put into them. If you have two friends with birthdays close together, and you buy them exactly the same thing, the gifts won't seem as personal or well thought out.

Is it OK to exchange a gift?

If the person who gave you the gift is never going to know anything about it, then it would be fine. But many shops need a receipt before they'll exchange something, and besides, you might not even know which shop the present came from in the first place. Therefore, you'll need to talk to the person who gave you the present, so think carefully about how they might feel. If someone gives you clothes or shoes that are the wrong size, a video game that's the wrong format or something else that you couldn't get any use out of, they couldn't possibly object if you swapped it for the same thing in the right size, format or whatever.

If you want to exchange something because you already have one the same, it's fair enough, but remember that the person who gave it to you could feel a bit disappointed, so be extra gentle with them, and make a big thing about how clever they were to know your taste so well. Exchanging something simply because you don't like it is a far dodgier area. If you think you can get away with a white lie, then go ahead. Your best bet is something like 'I went back to change it for the right size but they didn't have any more, so I got this instead'. If fibs are inappropriate (say, the gift was a hand-knitted pyjama case), you're probably stuck with it.

If someone buys you an outrageously expensive present, does that mean you have to spend more the next time you give them a present? If you can't afford to, should you tell them?

You should never spend more on a present than you can afford, or more than you want to spend. There's no need to talk about it – the easiest way to say let's not get each other expensive presents, is to give a cheaper gift when it comes to your turn. As long as you seemed wildly appreciative of the thing you were given, the extravagant gift giver won't think you're ungrateful. If they do, they're not very bright.

How soon is it OK to give gifts to someone you're dating?

There's no hard and fast rule, but it's worth being cautious, as giving someone a gift after you've only been on a few dates can seem like you're coming on a bit too strong. Birthday gifts are OK early on as long as they're not too extravagant. So are casual presents – such as a book, CD or video game of yours that you've chatted about, or your date's favourite chocolate bar. If you're going to give anything more romantic – whether it's flowers or something expensive – be aware that you're saying, 'I'm quite serious about you . . .'. Your date might be overjoyed, or they might be spooked and wish that you'd slow down a little – or back off altogether.

Out and About

Going to the Cinema

Unless you want to leave the cinema with everyone thinking that you're a first-class idiot, you should always stick with good cinema protocol. Here it is:

- If someone wants to get past you, it's not enough to tuck your feet daintily under the chair and suck in your stomach – a certain amount of climbing and clambering will still have to go on. If you really want to be helpful, stand up. It won't kill you.

- If you've got any food that needs unwrapping, do it before the film starts, and eat as quietly as you can. The sound of someone frantically picking at plastic, crinkling foil, munching crisps or popping bubble gum bubbles is a major irritation for everyone else.

- You can get away with putting your feet up on the seats in front of you only if there is no one sitting in them.

- Like your mum always said: Sit still, for goodness' sake! Bobbing around and shifting position a million times is annoying for people sitting behind you. Kicking against the chair in front is even worse. And in some kinds of cinema seats, leg jiggling can be felt by everyone in your row of seats and might cause mass panic that there is an impending earth tremor.

- The tradition of making out in the back row is a good one. Of course, you can sit in the back row and not kiss, but if you want to pull, the back row is the best place. Not only do you have more privacy, but more importantly, you won't be blocking anyone's view. People are unlikely to mind as long as you do it quietly, and as far away from everyone else as possible. It's also worth mentioning that some movies are not ideal for this. If you make out during films that are moving or tragic, which other people are taking dead seriously, someone is bound to get cross. Smooching your way through anything involving 9/11 or the holocaust, for example, is not a top idea.

- Talking in the cinema will not make you popular. As soon as the lights go down, all general chat should stop. Making loud, rude comments about how rubbish the adverts are is perfectly acceptable – everyone does it. But once the film is on, keep quiet.

- Turn your mobile off! And no, switching it onto silent or vibrate doesn't count since you shouldn't even think about answering a call or reading or writing a text – even if there's no noise, the light coming from your screen is really distracting – you don't need to have it on at all.

- If someone else is yakking, unwrapping things, using their mobile or doing anything else that is spoiling your enjoyment of the film, feel free to hiss a loud 'Shhh!' or 'Turn your phone off!' in their direction.

- Going to the loo in the cinema does disturb everyone else a little bit, but that doesn't mean it's rude – I mean, if you've got to go, you've got to go. Get up quietly, say 'Excuse me' as you climb over people (and 'Sorry' if you stomp on them, or stick your foot in their box of popcorn), and make your way up or down the aisle nice and swiftly, with your head ducked down low. You should also make a point of counting the rows on your way to the toilet, so you don't have to spend twenty minutes hunting high and low for your seat when you come back.

Going to Gigs, Concerts and the Theatre

What should you do if you find someone else sitting in your seat?

Stay calm. In these situations, it almost never turns out that two people actually have the same ticket, so it's bound to be a mistake – either the person in the seat has got mixed up about the seat numbers, or you have. Your best bet is to ignore the person in the seat, find an usher immediately and let them deal with it – that's their job. They can check both the tickets and sort the situation out without anyone getting stroppy.

Queues

If you're with a big group of people at a funfair or theme park, is it OK for one person to stand in a queue for a ride and have the others join them when they get to the front?

In theory, it's fair. But it depends on how many of you there are, and what the queue looks like. Groups of more than about six should definitely have more than one person queuing. And you should think twice about doing it at all if the queue area is enclosed somehow. Why? Because the mates of the person in the queue will have to push past people who have been queuing for years to get to the front, and that always gets people's backs up – for all they know, there's some serious queue-jumping going on. If the front of the queue is easily accessible, you're less likely to annoy people.

159

If you're queuing up to buy something, is it OK for one person to save a place in the queue for others?

Only if you all pay together and sort it out between yourselves afterwards. If you all pay separately, the people in line behind you have to wait an extra-long time before their turn, which isn't fair.

How about if it's just one person you want to save a place in the queue for. Is that OK?

It's slightly more acceptable, but they should always join you in the queue well before you reach the front. Otherwise, it's very frustrating for the people behind you in the queue to think, 'Oh good, I'm next' and then have your friend jump in ahead of them.

What should you do if someone pushes into a queue ahead of you?

Point to the end of the queue and tell them politely that that's the end of the queue. If they ignore you, tap them on the shoulder and say in a friendly but firm way, 'Excuse me – I was ahead of you'.

Doors

Are boys still supposed to open doors for girls, or is it sexist?

People don't open doors because they assume that other people can't – they do it as a friendly, helpful or respectful gesture, so, no, it's not sexist.

Today's door-rules apply to people of both sexes. They are:

- If you want to open a door for someone – anyone – go ahead and do it; it's a nice thing to do.
- If you don't want to, you don't have to, although you should never just go striding blithely through a heavy door and then let it slam back into someone's face!
- You should always hold a door open for anyone who might actually need it. That includes people in wheelchairs, people with their hands full (because they're carrying or pushing things) and people who might find the door heavy (little kids, old people, pregnant women, people who look tired or a bit weedy).

Getting Around

Who should get to use the door of a train or bus first – the people getting on, or the people getting off?

The people getting off. This really makes sense, because if the getting-on people use the door first, it's hard for them to get past the getting-off people and into the bus or train, and the getting-off people have to fight to get out.

I once offered my seat on the bus to an old lady, and she got annoyed and said there was nothing wrong with her. It's not rude to offer an old person your seat, is it?

Far from it! Offering someone your seat – for any reason – is very nice. The only person being rude was her.

Are men still supposed to offer their seats to ladies, or is that sexist and old-fashioned?

Yes. But then, it's unlikely that any female would actually complain or be offended if a guy offered her his seat – in fact, she'd probably be delighted! However, there are some people who everyone – male or female – should offer to give up their seat to. They are:
• Old people
• Pregnant women
• Anyone carrying lots of bags, or something heavy
• Anyone holding a baby or little kid
• Anyone who appears to be having trouble standing up!

Why do some people give me dirty looks when I use my mobile on the bus?

I can't say for sure, unless you happen to be the bus driver – that would explain everything. Seriously, though, as long as you're not in a phone-free carriage on a train, using your mobile on public transport is technically a perfectly OK thing to do. But there are some guidelines to follow if you want to avoid getting the evil eye from your fellow passengers:
• Turn your mobile onto vibrate, especially if you've got an annoying ringtone!
• Keep your voice as quiet as you can – astonishing as it may seem, not everyone on the bus or train is desperate to hear a blow-by-blow account of what happened in double-science yesterday.
• Even if you're talking quietly, avoid saying anything that might shock or offend nearby old folk or parents with younger kids – it's hard to judge how audible your conversation is, so it's better to be careful.
• If possible, try not to spend the entire journey talking on

the phone – if someone is finding your chatting annoying for whatever reason, it's nice to give them a bit of a break, especially on the bus or on a crowded train, where they don't have the option of moving further away from you if they're getting irritated.

Don't you think it's rude for people to ask you to turn your i-Pod down when you're using public transport? After all, it's only a teeny, weeny little bit of noise that comes out when you have it up loud?

Yes, it's a teeny, weeny noise, but it's a teeny, weeny annoying noise, so the answer is no, it's not rude – it's fair enough. If you love having your MP3 player on turbo-blast, try putting a hat on over your ears to muffle the noise emissions, and try to sit as far away from people as possible, or next to other people wearing headphones!

This rule applies to hand-held games, too. Ideally, you should turn the sound off completely if you're playing in public, or plug in a headset (with the sound turned down low). Those beeps and blips might be tiny, but if you're not the one playing the game, they're a mighty pain in the backside.

If someone tries to chat to you on the bus or train, is it rude not to talk to them?

Not at all. Strangers who start up conversations are invading your privacy, and therefore they have to be prepared to get the brush-off. If you fancy a chat, fine. If not, don't worry about it.

But surely you can't just ignore them?

You could ignore them, but it's best just to smile, answer whatever comment they made to you in as few words as possible and then pretend to get very interested in looking out of the window – they'll soon get the message.

Being Late

How long should you wait for someone who is late?

If you haven't heard from them, and you can't get through to their mobile to find out where they are and how long they expect to be (or they don't have a mobile, or you don't have their number, or whatever), then there's an unwritten rule that you should wait about twenty minutes. But of course, you don't have to stick to it! Hanging around alone is horrible, and if you want to leave sooner, feel free – being late is rude, and your friend or date wouldn't have any real right to complain. If you want to wait longer than twenty minutes, that's fair enough, but hanging around for any longer than half an hour shows a distinct lack of self-respect. This is bad news, because it gives people the impression that you don't care if they treat you like dirt and walk all over you.

If you decide not to wait for someone who is late, you should phone their home as soon as possible and leave them a friendly message explaining that you waited however long and then gave up. If you don't do this, things can get confusing.

What should you do if you're late to meet a friend or a date, you haven't been able to get hold of them, and when you arrive, they're not there?

To avoid this kind of situation, it's always better to leave yourself more time than you think you'll need to get anywhere, and call or text as soon as you think you might be running a bit late. But even so, unforeseen mix-ups do happen. If you're less than twenty minutes late, wait for a bit – after all, they might be late too and actually not have arrived yet! If you're fairly sure that they've been and gone, call them right away and leave a grovelling message. If it's a date (rather than a friend) that you were supposed to be meeting, you should work extra hard to make amends – remember that as far as they can see it, you stood them up. So keep calling until you get hold of them, and make it clear that you're very sorry and you'd like to arrange another date.

Should you tell someone off for being late?

If they're less than ten minutes late, no. If they're more than ten minutes late, listen to their excuse, then decide. If it sounds like a feeble excuse, or they're always late, tell them off. Once you've made your feelings known, though, drop the subject and don't sulk – you've made your point, and no one wants to hang out with a sulker. The best way to knock a serial latecomer into shape is not to wait for them. If they know that you're always going to be there, waiting patiently, they're bound to do it again. They're far more likely to pull their socks up next time if they turn up to find you gone.

Tipping

A tip is a little extra payment for someone who has done something for you. The following are all people you might come across who expect a tip:

Waiters and Waitresses

- Waiters and waitresses everywhere expect a tip, from big, posh restaurants, to little, tiny cafés – even if you're just having a cup of tea. There's no law to say that you have to leave a tip, but you always should, because waiters and waitresses usually get paid extremely badly, and rely on tips to bump up their wages.
- The only time you can consider not leaving a tip is if you thought the service was really terrible (say, if your food took ages and ages to arrive, the orders were all wrong or the serving person was very rude).
- Sometimes, the tip is already added for you. If you can see the words *service charge*, *service* or *gratuity* written before an amount of money on the bill, you just pay the total amount at the bottom of the bill and you're sorted – you don't need to leave any extra.
- If the bill isn't itemised (i.e. it just has the total figure written on it), or there is no bill at all (you're just told how much to pay), ask the person who served you whether service is included.
- If the tip isn't included in your bill, you need to work out how much to leave. People usually give between twelve and fifteen per cent of the total price. Fifteen per cent is usual in big cities – and in posher places twenty per cent isn't unheard of – but you can get away with twelve per cent (or even ten) elsewhere, or if the total charge was quite small.

- You don't need to hand the tip directly to your serving person – just leave it on the table, or add it in with the rest of the money you're paying. In places where you get up and pay at a till, you'll often find a little bowl or jar with a note saying *service* or *tips* or just *thank you*, in which case you pop the money in there.

- Occasionally, if you've paid in cash and you're only owed a smallish amount of change, a waiter or waitress will assume that you want to leave all of it as a tip. They should-n't do this – it's entirely up to you to decide how much you want to tip – so if you don't get given change, you've got every right to ask for it.

- At coffee bars, where you order your food and drinks at the counter and take them to the table yourself, you're not obliged to leave a tip at all. But if someone has made you a special-order coffee just the way you like it (perhaps a cap-puccino with three centimetres of coffee and ten centimetres of froth!) or you've left a huge mess on your table, it's nice to drop fifty pence, or whatever you can afford, in the tip box by the till.

Cloakroom Attendants

- If there is a charge for leaving your coat or jacket some-where, you don't need to worry about tipping as well. But if the service appears to be free, you'll always find a bowl for tips, and you should always leave one. The right amount is usually between fifty pence and a pound, depending on where you are, but it's worth checking the bowl: if it seems to be full of pound coins, you should definitely leave a pound. In smaller places, the bowl might have mainly twenty pences in it, which would let you know that twenty pence is an OK amount to leave. By the way, you should never help yourself to change from a tip bowl. If you don't have the right amount, ask for change.

Toilet Attendants

- Some public loos and loos in restaurants have a person sitting around in them, who makes sure they're kept clean. They usually leave out a little saucer for tips. They won't give you a hard time if you don't tip, but if you can, it's nice to leave between ten pence and fifty pence.

Taxi and Mini-cab Drivers

- Drivers always expect a tip, and can often get quite stroppy if you don't leave one. You should tip roughly ten per cent or fifteen per cent of the fare, but it doesn't need to be exact – most people just suggest that the driver keeps the change (as long as it's not far too little), or round up to the nearest pound.

Barbers

- If you live in a small town, you should leave about a pound, maybe two. In a city, you should leave roughly ten to fifteen per cent of the total charge for your haircut.

Hairdressers

- You're expected to tip around ten to fifteen per cent of the total price you paid. This goes to the hairdresser, and you usually hand it to them directly. If this seems too embarrassing, you can ask the person at the reception desk who takes your money to do it for you – you just pay your bill, sort out the tip and ask, 'Would you mind giving this to (hairdresser's name) for me, please?'. Don't worry, they'll know what it's for! If your hair was not shampooed by the hairdresser, but by a junior, you should give them something as well – usually about a pound. If the junior did anything else for you – like handing the hairdresser curlers for a perm, or foil for doing highlights, you should give them an extra fifty pence or a pound. If a different junior did this, you should tip them the same. If you can't find them, give their tip to your hairdresser to give to them (or leave it at reception).

- One more thing (phew, nothing like a relaxing trip to the hairdressers, eh?): some salon owners don't accept tips, so if it was the owner who did your hair, you should ask them or the receptionist if they do before you get your cash out.

Beauticians

- If you're having any kind of treatment – leg-waxing, a manicure, whatever – you should tip between ten per cent and fifteen per cent of the total price.

Here's how to work out percentages if you're not much cop at maths:
- Working out ten per cent is easy: you just move the decimal point back one space and drop the last number – so if your bill was fifteen pounds, ten per cent would be one pound fifty.
- Fifteen per cent isn't too much harder. Just figure out ten per cent, as above, then figure out what is half of that number. Add that to the ten per cent figure, and you're there! So, fifteen per cent of fifteen pounds would be roughly two pounds and twenty-five pence (one pound fifty plus seventy-five pence). It's much simpler than it sounds, honest!

Work and Interviews

Interviews

What should you wear to an interview?

Whether you're going for an interview with the head of a new school or college, or for a job, you should choose clothes that are clean and neatly-ironed, in good condition (not fraying, ripped or stained) and which go together well (no clashing colours or weird combinations). Avoid clothes that are slobby, sporty, sexy or hyper-trendy (unless you're going for a job somewhere particularly cool or fashion-oriented), and don't forget to apply the same rules when you're choosing your footwear.

If you're going for a job and the advert is very casual and just asks you to apply for the job in person, it's still a good idea to avoid really scruffy clothes. Even though for casual jobs (such as a newspaper boy/girl) you wouldn't need to look smart, you'll always make a better impression and so be more likely to get the job in the first place.

What else should you know about interviews?

Plenty! Here you go:
- Always arrive on time, or a few minutes early. I mean, if you can't be punctual for the interview, the chances of you arriving on time for work don't look too good, do they?
- Be polite and friendly to everyone you meet – if the receptionist or another employee or student reports that you were rude or snotty, you'll damage your chances, even if you were charming in the interview. Employers know

that everyone puts on their best face for interviews, and will assume that the nasty stuff is the real you.

- When the interviewer greets you, stand up and stick your hand out to shake hands. Always try to give a firm, confident handshake. And remember that the friendlier and more enthusiastic you seem, the better a first impression you'll make.
- Don't sit down until the interviewer invites you to.
- If the interviewer has a desk, don't dump stuff on it. If you need to give or show something to the person interviewing you, hand it to them directly. If you're handing them something unprompted (in other words, they haven't asked you for it), you should explain what it is (e.g. 'These are my letters of recommendation') – don't just shove it at them.
- Usually, the interviewer will steer the course of the interview, so listen to what they have to say, and answer their questions before you ask any of your own. Ideally, you should wait until you're asked if you have any questions, but if you need something explained, or have a small question as you go along, it's fine to pipe up before, as long as you wait until there's a natural break – don't interrupt!
- Save questions about wages, holidays and perks until near the end of the interview.
- Some people are scared to blow their own trumpet in interviews because they're worried that bragging would sound rude and big-headed. However, it makes no sense to put yourself down, or even just stay quiet about your abilities and qualities when you're trying to persuade someone to give you a job! Bragging is fine, as long as you're bragging about specific facts, like your grades, your qualifications, things you've done, good qualities that you believe you have or things people have said about you. The only brags you should avoid are silly, over-the-top ones that are just your opinion, like 'I'm the best person for the job!'

(how do you know when you don't know anything about the other people who have applied!?) or 'If you don't employ me, you'll be missing a great opportunity!' (This not only sounds like a threat – and no one likes a threat – but also as if you've got an ego the size of a small planet.)

- If the interviewer has to take a phonecall or talk to someone while you're there, you should pretend not to listen to what they're saying (pretend to read something, rummage through your bag – anything!). Then act like you didn't hear a word of the conversation. Why? Because most people would rather employ someone who respects their privacy than a nosy parker!

- It's up to the interviewer to decide when the interview finishes – you should never end it yourself. Although the interviewer probably won't say, 'Right, the interview is finished now!', it's not hard to pick up the cues – they may talk about what will happen next ('We'll be in contact soon', 'We've got a lot more people to see'), or 'Thank you for coming in', and they might stand up. Once they've signalled that the interview is finished, that's it – you should thank them, get up and go. Don't try to ask any more questions – especially not, 'So, how did I do?' or 'Have I got the job?/Have I got a place?'.

Looking for Work

It's always nice to know exactly what to do in a situation, and understand what's expected of you, but when you're looking for work, it's essential. If you're jumpy, horribly confused, or simply clueless about what to do, you could bungle the whole thing. If you can remember these useful pointers, though, you'll have the best possible chance of getting the job.

What should you say when you call about a job you've read or heard about?

First, don't assume that the person who answers the phone is there to tell you all about it. If you just plunge in and start gabbing on about the job, it's quite likely that you'll be bending the ear of someone who knows nothing about it, who will have to interrupt you and hand you over to someone else – not a great start, eh? So what do you do instead? Well, it's quite common to kick off by saying, 'I'm calling about the job', but it can sound a bit brash, and it's far more impressive and polite to ask, 'May I speak to someone concerning the job vacancy, please?' It's also a good idea to be specific about which job you're applying for – there may be more than one kind of position going.

Secondly, don't forget that this is your first chance to impress, so don't muck it up by being dozy or annoying. To make a good impression, you should basically be polite, and keep the call as short as possible by only asking good questions. 'Has the job been taken?' or 'Is the post still vacant?' is the most important one. If the job is still going, you can also ask for certain pieces of essential info if – and only if – you can't find them in the advert (you should try to find a copy before you call). That kind of info would include:

- Whether applicants need to be within a certain age range.
- Whether you need any specific qualifications or experience.
- What name and address your application should be sent to, or whether it should be done by email.

Don't ask any more questions, or you'll be keeping your prospective employers on the phone for way too long, which won't win you any brownie points. And don't ask about wages. Save that subject, and any other questions, for when you (hopefully) get an interview.

What makes a good job application?

The key word here is effort. The more effort you put in, the better an impression you'll make.

- If you're applying by post, always write your application letter on a computer and print it out on plain, good-quality, A4 paper.
- Spell well (always use spell-check), use good English and try not to make any mistakes. (This is best done by getting someone else to proofread your letter for you before you print out the final copy.)
- Be respectful. This means using people's titles and surnames (i.e. *Dear Ms So-and-so, I spoke with Mr So-and-so at your office the other day . . .*). If you need to mention someone whose name you don't know, refer to them as *the gentleman/lady I spoke with . . .*, or *your colleague.* Being respectful also means saying only positive things about the business that you are applying for a job at. (So if you're applying for a job at The Kwick-Kebab Hut, don't write: *I hope to eventually work in a proper restaurant, but . .*).
- Include all the information that your prospective employer might need. That includes your personal details (full name, age, address and phone number), your qualifications and work experience (if any), and maybe a brief reason why you think that you and this job were made for each other.
- Keep the letter as short as possible. It takes time to wade through job applications, and if your letter is extra long and rambling, you're wasting your prospective employer's time – which is not exactly what you call getting off to a flying start.
- Attach or enclose a well-written curriculum vitae (cv).

Getting Down to Business

Work is one area where manners are even more important than usual if you want to get ahead. If yours are not up to much, you're not likely to get far, and you might even lose your job altogether. If they're good, you'll get results – your employers will be more loyal to you, you'll get good recommendations and you might even get more money, if you're lucky. Here are a few basic hints for the most common teenage jobs.

Babysitting

- Arrive on time. If you're late, you might totally mess up your employers' plans for the evening – not a great start.
- If you get given a long, dull lecture ('Here are our mobile numbers, please can you keep the dog out of the bedroom, don't forget that Jack likes his bottle warmed up to exactly 37.5 degrees, blah blah blah'), listen carefully, nod politely and repeat the instructions back to show that you've understood them (rather than yawning and saying, 'Yeah yeah yeah, whatever . . .).
- Even when you've got the place to yourself, show a bit of respect. Babysitters who chat on the landline, snoop around, raid the fridge, ignore the kids, and invite friends or dates round always get found out and rarely get employed again.
- You'll get extra points for politely taking phone messages and tidying things up a bit if you get the chance. And if your employers come back drunk as skunks, don't mention it unless they offer to drive you home, in which case it's fine to ask for a taxi instead – when it comes to your safety, you can forget about manners!

Washing Cars

- You can't go too far wrong here as long as you do the job well and avoid making personal comments – no one wants to hear your opinion on what a useless driver they must be to get so many dents in the bodywork, or any little quips about how you'd heard that the council had opened a new municipal dump, but hadn't realised that it was located in their back seat.

Paper Rounds

- When you're on a paper round, remember that you're representing your employer. In other words, if you wind people up, your employer could get some stick from them, which certainly won't win you any brownie points, and could even cost you your job. To avoid winding people up, you should always be cheerful, polite and friendly to the folk you're delivering to. If your delivery round is early in the morning, you should do everything as quietly as possible, so as not to wake anyone up. And if you're on a bike, you should ride carefully, being very thoughtful to other road and pavement-users – especially if you're wearing or carrying something that identifies your employer!

Working in a Shop

- If you're old enough to work in a shop (i.e. over sixteen) don't forget the old saying: The customer is always right. This doesn't actually mean that the customer *is* always right – in fact, the customer is often actually a crotchety, unreasonable jerk. It just means that you have to act like they're right, because if you don't, they can take their custom elsewhere, which won't make your employers very happy. Apart from pretending that they're right all the time, you also have to be very polite to the customers – the more smiles, good mornings, pleases and thank yous you can slip in, the more popular you'll be with your boss.

Work Experience

- The sad reality of being on work experience is that you can end up getting given a lot of the less interesting tasks that no one else wants to do, and don't get paid a penny for it. Still, it's worth making an effort to be polite and likeable at your place of work, because who knows – one day you might want to apply for a full-time job there, and a popular work-experiencer will have a better chance of getting the job than someone who nobody knows, and an unpopular one won't have a chance at all. Even if you never apply for a job there, you can ask your employers to write you a reference – and a glowing reference is a very handy thing to have. So here's the deal: a good work-experiencer never whinges, always asks if there's anything they can do for anyone, doesn't hassle people when they're busy and never demands to do more interesting jobs than the ones they're given. Nightmarish, yes, but well worth doing!

And Finally . . .

I've tried to cover every common situation and topic – and quite a few less common ones, too – but you never know what challenges could be lurking around the corner. The great thing about life is that it's full of surprises, but that also means that you sometimes find yourself unprepared, and, believe me, even the most self-assured adults sometimes find themselves unsure of the right thing to do!

Whatever situation you may find yourself in, all you really need to remember are these three tips:

1. Copy!
If you're not the only one in the situation, always take a moment to sneak a look at how everyone else is handling it. Or, more specifically, focus on just one person who looks like they know what they're doing, and follow their lead!

2. Ask!
Never be afraid to tell someone that you're not sure what to do. I guarantee you that no one is going to laugh, be shocked that you asked, or think any the less of you.

3. Make it up!
When all else fails, take a wild guess! As long as nothing you do makes anyone else feel uncomfortable, the chances are that it'll be near enough to the right thing, or it doesn't really matter if it isn't! Whatever you do, do it with confidence and a friendly attitude and you won't go far wrong.

☆

www.piccadillypress.co.uk

☆ The latest news on forthcoming books

☆ Chapter previews

☆ Author biographies

☆ Fun quizzes

☆ Reader reviews

☆ Competitions and fab prizes

☆ Book features and cool downloads

☆ And much, much more . . .

Log on and check it out!

Piccadilly Press